CHILDREN'S RIGHTS IN THE BALANCE

CHILDREN'S RIGHTS IN THE BALANCE

THE PARTICIPATION – PROTECTION DEBATE

Kathleen Marshall

Funded by the Calouste Gulbenkian Foundation

EDINBURGH: THE STATIONERY OFFICE

© The Stationery Office Limited 1997

The Stationery Office Limited
South Gyle Crescent, Edinburgh EH12 9EB

Application for reproduction should be made to The Stationery Office Limited
First published 1997

British Library Cataloguing in Publication Data

A catalogue record for this book is available from the British Library

ISBN 0 11 495852 1

Contents

ACKNOWLEDGEMENTS

I am indebted to a number of people for allowing me to intrude upon their own well-filled timetables to fill in my questionnaire and often to talk to me about children's rights to participate. Others contributed by commenting upon the draft. In particular, I would like to record my appreciation of the support of the Calouste Gulbenkian Foundation who generously funded this research.

The following names are set out in alphabetical order only.

Professor Stewart Asquith
Paul Curno
Harriet Dempster
Anne Hall Dick
Professor Sandford Fox
Dorothy Gallagher
Greg Gallagher
Cathy Jamieson and the young people of Who Cares? Scotland
Sheriff Brian Kearney
Sheriff David Kelbie
Gerison Lansdown
Carol Loch
Maureen Lynch
Sandra McDerment
Susie McKillop
Hugh Mackintosh
Peter Newell
Christina del Priore
Barbara Reid
Malcolm Schaeffer
Anne Stafford
Ruth Stark
Kay Tisdall
Deirdre Watson

About the Author

Kathleen Marshall qualified as a solicitor in 1975 and worked initially in local government in Glasgow. In 1989 she was appointed Director of the Scottish Child Law Centre, a post she held for 5 years.

She is currently a consultant in child law and Visiting Professor to Glasgow University's Centre for the Child & Society. She serves on a number of bodies concerned with the rights and interests of children.

Her consultancy work has addressed issues such as support for children and families and child protection. She was legal consultant to the Consortium for the Children (Scotland) Bill which was convened by Children in Scotland and the Scottish Child Law Centre and which lobbied successfully on many aspects of what became the Children (Scotland) Act 1995.

Chapter 1

◆

INTRODUCTION

John is 14 years old and wants to know who his father is. His mother won't say. He believes there is something in his social work file about it and he wants to see the file. His home life is troubled and decisions are being made about his welfare. He feels unhappy because it seems that there is some information about him that everyone knows except him. He wants to know.

John was conceived as a result of a violent rape. His natural father is in a facility for the criminally insane. Should John be told?

Jennifer is 10. Her parents have decided to divorce. They both want Jennifer to live with them. As they cannot agree, it is likely that the matter will end up in court. The court may wish to find out Jennifer's views. The parents know this and Jennifer knows it, too. She loves both her parents and would rather continue to live with them both. If that is not possible, she has some views about what she wants to happen, but she does not want to hurt anyone's feelings.

How can Jennifer best be involved in this decision?

A meeting has been convened to discuss the future of 11-year-old Matthew. His single-parent mother has an erratic lifestyle and sometimes neglects him. Matthew is living with foster carers. He is attached to his mother but does not want to live with her. His social worker explains Matthew's views to the meeting. His mother becomes emotional and says that, if that is the case, she never wants to see or hear from him again. She later calms down and retracts this statement, but Matthew was present and heard it.

1

Should Matthew have been present? Were there other ways his views could have been taken into account?

Most adults have an instinctive desire to protect children from situations and information which might cause them distress. This has been reflected over the past century in an increase in legal and welfare mechanisms aiming to identify and address their needs.

Increasingly, expected standards of behaviour in relation to children have been translated into the language of rights, with the child as the subject. Rights based on protection from harm have been relatively uncontroversial. When, in 1979, the United Nations set about drafting a new Convention on the Rights of the Child, it took earlier protective formulations as its starting point, but introduced a radical innovation; children, it said, should have a right to participate in decisions affecting them.

On being informed of this right, the first reaction of many adults is one of misunderstanding. Participation is understood as a power to control. In fact, the Convention does not give children autonomy. The right to participate does entail the power to influence, but it involves making a contribution to the decision-making process, rather than controlling it. The right to participate is balanced by a continuing emphasis on the right to be protected.

The balance is not always an easy one. There can be a tension between respect for children's right to participate, and their right to have their interests protected. This resolves around two issues:

- the development of participation mechanisms appropriate to children; and
- consideration of whether an invitation to participate might in itself be against the child's interests in any circumstances.

This book explores the meaning and implications of the relevant articles of the Convention, looks at attitudes towards them and attempts to respond to them, and then assesses these in the light of the Convention itself. The focus is on decisions which affect children's personal lives rather than involvement in political or organisational decision-making processes. The final chapter seeks to identify a framework for participation which will achieve an appropriate balance with the right to protection.

1.1 Methodology

The analysis of the debates surrounding drafting of the Convention was based upon a study of the published *Guide to the Travaux Préparatoires*.[1]

Comment upon the progress of various states in implementing the relevant articles of the Convention was based upon study of the states' initial reports to the UN Committee on the Rights of the Child, proceedings of the Committee, and their concluding observations and recommendations. This means that the law of any country is presented as it was at the time the state submitted its report.

States selected for inclusion in this book were those whose reports to the Committee led to discussion and/or comment about the application of Article 12 or its relationship with Article 3.

Analysis of the European Convention on the Exercise of Children's Rights was based upon critical reading of the document and the accompanying explanatory report.

Chapter 5 on attitudes to participation of children was based upon a small-scale survey and individual interviews. A group of four young people with experience of the child-care system was included in this process.

The draft typescript was the circulated for comment to selected individuals in the UK and abroad.

The final conclusions draw upon all of the above, together with the particular perspective of the author, a Scottish solicitor with a particular interest in, and experience of, issues relating to the rights of children.

Notes

1. Detrick S., Ed. (1991), *The United Nations Convention on the Rights of the Child – a Guide to the 'Travaux Préparatoires'*, Martinus Nijhoff, Dordrecht.

Chapter 2

◆

THE UNITED NATIONS CONVENTION ON THE RIGHTS OF THE CHILD

2.1 Introduction

In 1978 the Polish Government proposed to the UN Human Rights Commission the drafting of a Convention on the Rights of the Child. The Commission responded by setting up a Working Group which considered, consulted on and amended a draft convention submitted by Poland. After ten years' work, the Convention on the Rights of the Child was passed by the General Assembly of the United Nations in November 1989. It has since been ratified by over 170 states. Ratification commits states to bringing their law, policy and practice into line with the standards set by the Convention. Implementation is monitored by an international committee of experts to whom states must report two years after ratification and every five years thereafter.

The articles of interest in this book are Articles 3 and 12. Article 3 states that:

1. In all actions concerning children, whether undertaken by public or private social welfare institutions, courts of law, administrative authorities or legislative bodies, the best interests of the child shall be a primary consideration.
2. States Parties undertake to ensure the child such protection and care as is necessary for his or her well-being, taking into account the rights and duties of his or her parents, legal guardians, or other individuals legally responsible for him or her, and, to this end, shall take all appropriate legislative and administrative measures.

Article 12 states that:

1. States Parties shall assure to the child who is capable of forming his or her own views the right to express those views freely in all matters

affecting the child, the views of the child being given due weight in accordance with the age and maturity of the child.

2. For this purpose, the child shall in particular be provided the opportunity to be heard in any judicial and administrative proceedings affecting the child, either directly, or through a representative or an appropriate body, in a manner consistent with the procedural rules of national law.[1]

For the purposes of the Convention, a child is any person under 18 years of age, unless the age of majority in a particular state is lower, in which case the lower age applies.

What do these articles mean? What considerations shaped their final form? Did the drafters consider the internal tensions between these articles, and, if so, how did they seek to resolve them? In order to answer these questions it is necessary to look at the earlier statements of the rights of children which formed the starting point for the UN Convention, and the drafting of the Convention itself.

2.2 The Conceptual Development of Children's Rights

The first international recognition of children's rights came in 1924. In that year, the Assembly of the League of Nations passed the Declaration of the Rights of the Child. This five-point document, known as the Declaration of Geneva, stated:

By the present Declaration of the Rights of the Child, commonly known as the 'Declaration of Geneva', men and women of all nations, recognising that mankind owes to the child the best it has to give, declare and accept it as their duty that, beyond and above all considerations of race, nationality or creed:

1. The child must be given the means needed for its normal development, both materially and spiritually.
2. The child that is hungry should be fed; the child that is sick should be helped; the erring child should be reclaimed; and the orphan and the homeless child should be sheltered and succoured.
3. The child must be first to receive relief in times of distress.
4. The child must be put in a position to earn a livelihood and must be protected against every form of exploitation.
5. The child must be brought up in the consciousness that its best qualities are to be used in the service of its fellow men.[2]

The rights proclaimed are relatively specific, although 'the means needed for its normal development' would require interpretation and application to specific circumstances.

The next development was the passing of the UN's 1948 Declaration on the Rights of the Child. This was a seven-point statement, heavily influenced by its predecessor. It stated that:

> By the present Declaration of the Rights of the Child, commonly known as the Declaration of Geneva, men and women of all nations, recognising that Mankind owes the Child the best that it has to give, declare and accept it as their duty to meet this obligation in all respects:
>
> I. THE CHILD must be protected beyond and above all considerations of race, nationality or creed.
> II. THE CHILD must be cared for with due respect for the family as an entity.
> III. THE CHILD must be given means requisite for its normal development, materially, morally and spiritually.
> IV. THE CHILD that is hungry must be fed; the child that is sick must be nursed; the child that is physically or mentally handicapped must be helped; the maladjusted child must be re-educated; the orphan and the waif must be sheltered and succoured.
> V. THE CHILD must be first to receive relief in times of distress.
> VI. THE CHILD must enjoy the full benefits provided by social welfare and social security schemes; the child must receive a training which will enable it, at the right time, to earn a livelihood, and must be protected against every form of exploitation.
> VII. THE CHILD must be brought up in the consciousness that its talents must be devoted to the service of its fellowmen.[3]

The concerns of the time can be seen reflected in the fact that:

- race, nationality and creed have been given a higher profile;
- it was felt necessary to emphasise the need for respect for the family as an entity;
- physical and mental handicaps receive a specific mention;
- 'erring' children are displaced in favour of 'maladjusted' children;
- reference is made to social welfare and social security schemes; and
- reference to the ability to earn a livelihood is tempered by the qualification that this should be 'at the right time'.

The 1948 Declaration nevertheless shares with its predecessor an emphasis on the protective and developmental aspects.

In 1959 a new Declaration of the Rights of the Child further expanded the parameters. As well as being more wordy, it is recognised as introducing for the first time a reference to a right which is civil rather than predominantly protective in character. This is the right to a name and nationality.[4] It includes references to happiness, love and understanding. It asserts the child's right to play and to education, which is aimed at 'general culture' rather than related specifically to future employment.

The 1959 Declaration is also more specific and discriminating in its approach to the interests of the child. Whereas the earlier Declarations recognised that mankind owes the child 'the best it has to give', the 1959 document says that, in enacting laws concerning the protection and development of the child, the state is obliged to ensure that ' the best interests of the child shall be the paramount consideration'.[5] In contrast, those, including parents, who have responsibility for education and guidance of the child, are to regard the best interests of the child as 'the guiding principle'.[6]

The significance of this lies in the higher standard applied to the state. If an interest is 'paramount', it is 'of the greatest importance or significance; pre-eminent'.[7] A 'guiding' principle, on the other hand, is one which aims to 'advise or influence (a person) in his standards or opinions'.[8] The higher standard appears to have been attached to the narrower sphere of the law, and the lower, which admits of other considerations, to the wider sphere of parental education and guidance of children. This anticipates an important debate with regard to the standard to be applied to the interests of the child in what is now Article 3 of the 1989 United Nations Convention on the Rights of the Child.

2.3 The Drafting of the 1989 Convention – the Travaux Préparatoires

The Travaux Préparatoires are the preparatory workings of the drafters of the Convention. International law accords them a specific importance as an aid to interpretation of a treaty if the treaty's provisions are found to be unclear.[9] A *Guide to the Travaux Préparatoires* has been published, incorporating an overview of the drafting process and a compilation of those UN documents most helpful for an understanding of the thinking of the drafters, the debates entered into by them, and the compromises reached by them.[10]

The issue of compromise is raised again and again within these documents. The important, basic drafting work was undertaken by a Working Group on the Question of a Convention on the Rights of the Child. It was described as 'open-ended', signifying that any of the 43 states represented on the Commission on Human Rights could participate. Observer status was available to all other member states of the United Nations and to intergovernmental organisations. Observers were entitled to speak. Others could also participate with no right to speak, although they were often permitted to do so.

The Working Group operated on the basis of consensus; matters were never taken to a vote. Whilst this was important in securing a relatively trouble-free passage through the UN procedures, it did mean that the provisions of the Convention represented the minimum standard acceptable to all, rather than the ideal towards which many states would wish to strive. Indeed, the UN standards might be less satisfactory than those already in place in some states. This understanding is reflected in Article 41 of the Convention which states that:

> 41. Nothing in the present Convention shall affect any provisions which are more conducive to the realization of the rights of the child and which may be contained in:
>
> (a) The law of a State Party; or
> (b) International law in force for that State.

2.3.1 The Best Interests of the Child – Article 3 of the UN Convention

Debates about Article 3 centred on two main issues:

1. The level of priority to be given to the interests of the child as compared with other, competing interests.
2. The contexts in which this degree of priority should apply.

In order to understand this debate, note must be taken of the different levels of priority that were discussed. Children's interests were at different times posited as:

- the paramount consideration;
- the primary consideration;
- a primary consideration; or
- the guiding principle.

Where a child's interests were regarded as *paramount*, no other interests could be set up in opposition to them. The decision should reflect whatever served the child's interests, no matter what other interests might be affected.

Where a child's interests were *the primary consideration*, other interests might be taken into account, and might colour the decision, but the decision should still give precedence to the interests of the child.

Where a child's interests were reduced to *a primary consideration*, other interests might be judged so weighty as to outweigh those of the child, although the interests of the child must still be taken seriously into account.

The child's interest as *the guiding principle* is a statement with a less focused character.

The second issue concerns the scope of application of the principle. Could the same formulation be used for the actions of parents and carers and the actions of official bodies, or were these essentially different contexts, requiring different standards?

The first draft of the 1989 Convention echoed the 1959 Declaration in the precedence it accorded the best interests of the child. It also distinguished between parents and carers and official bodies. Official bodies enacting laws aimed at the protection and development of the child had to regard the child's best interests as 'the paramount consideration'. Parents and others responsible for the education and guidance of the child were to take the child's best interests as their 'guiding principle'.

The working group initially extended this to give children's interests a higher profile, resulting in the following formulation:

Article 3.1 In all actions concerning children, whether undertaken by their parents, guardians, social or state institutions, and in particular by courts of law and administrative authorities, the best interests of the child shall be the paramount consideration.

This removed the focus from law enactment to implementation and enforcement, and indeed to 'all actions', and extended the scope of paramountcy to parents, institutions and administrative authorities.

Whilst there was some support for the standard of paramountcy, others argued that children's interests could not be seen as overriding others in every case. Other parties might have 'equal or even superior legal interests in some cases (for example, medical emergencies during childbirth)'.[11] There was also criticism of attempts to regulate private, family decisions in the same way as official actions.

An amendment was submitted by the United States of America which sought both to reduce the scope of application of the principle and the precedence given to the interests of the child. It said that:

In all *official* actions concerning children, whether undertaken by public or private social welfare institutions, courts of law, or administrative authorities, the best interests of the child shall be *a primary consideration*. [Emphasis added.]

Parents were therefore taken out of the scope of the provision and the way was cleared for other considerations, apart from the interests of the child, to be taken into account.

This went further than many wanted. There was debate and further amendment. At one point the formulation was changed to '*the* primary consideration' as opposed to '*a* primary consideration'.[12] [Emphasis added.]

UNICEF, in its contribution to the technical review of the draft convention[13] argued strongly for the retention of a stronger formulation:

By stating that the child's best interests shall be 'a primary consideration' this provision uses what amounts to a twofold qualification. The word 'primary' implies that other considerations, although not deemed primary, may nevertheless be taken into account. The article 'a' indicates that there may be several considerations, each of which is primary. The issue which arises by virtue of standards incorporated in other widely-accepted human rights instruments is whether a single qualification is not sufficient. If this were considered to be the case, the wording could be changed to indicate that the child's best interests would be 'the primary consideration'.

However, as the *Guide to the Travaux Préparatoires* indicates:

> It was generally noted that there were situations in which the competing interest, *inter alia,* of justice and of society at large should be of at least equal, if not, greater importance than the interests of the child.[14]

It was noted that, where other instruments made the interests of the child *the* primary consideration, they were focused on more limited circumstances. It was suggested that the interests of the child could be made *the* primary consideration if the article was restricted to matters involving the welfare of the child. Faced with the options of reducing the scope of application in order to allow for a more intense focus on the interests of the child, the drafters preferred to retain the wider scope at the cost of diluting the duty. Ultimately it was agreed, in the spirit of compromise, that the American proposal be adopted, under deletion of the word 'official'.

Thus, the level of priority to be given to the interests of a child was lowered from 'the paramount consideration' to 'a primary consideration'. Despite later attempts by the Netherlands to reintroduce paramountcy, the final form of the Convention retained 'a primary consideration' as the standard to be applied.

With regard to the context in which this standard was to apply, the scope was widened to include matters not related to the protection or development of a child. States were to apply the standard truly to *all* actions concerning children, this extension being the justification for lowering the standard.

Reference to parents was thus omitted from Article 3.1. Article 18.1 introduces a new formulation for the responsibility of parents. Here it says that 'The best interests of the child will be their basic concern.'

2.3.2 The Child's Right to Express Views – Article 12 of the UN Convention

Article 12 consists of two paragraphs, which were placed together only at a late stage of drafting. Paragraph 1 sets out the general principle about the child's right to participate in all matters affecting the child, while paragraph 2 addresses the specific right of the child to be heard in judicial and administrative proceedings. The second paragraph was initially attached to Article 3 on the grounds that hearing a child was an essential part of the process of determining where the child's interests might lie.

Article 12 was an innovation of the 1989 Convention. None of the earlier children's rights documents had made specific reference to children's rights to express views and have them taken into account. Neither was it mentioned in the original draft convention submitted by Poland. The first intimations of its appearance can be found in the initial response by states to the Polish draft. The French response of 18 December 1978 observed:

> It would be desirable for the convention to include a provision affirming the right of the child at least to be consulted when certain events affecting his personal situation are to take place. The additional article might be worded as follows:
> As soon as the child is capable of understanding, his consent must be sought when decisions have to be taken that may seriously affect his personal situation, such as those relating to adoption or the granting of custody.[15]

Colombia's response to the draft noted that:

> Any plan or programme which a nation may adopt in relation to children should consider the child as an active and participating member of society in general and of a family in particular, so that his actions are not dissociated from the social environment in which he lives, and so that he is not regarded as an abstract subject alien to any objective reality.[16]

As a result of the consultation process, Poland submitted in 1979 a revised draft which contained the following:

> Article 7 [later renumbered to become Article 12]
> The State Parties to the present convention shall enable the child who is capable of forming his own views the right to express his opinion in matters concerning his own person, and in particular, marriage, choice of occupation, medical treatment, education and recreation.

Debate centred on the following points:

- whether states should be obliged to 'ensure' the right of the child to express opinions rather merely 'enable' it;

- whether there should be an obligation to give the child's views weight in accordance with the age and maturity of the child;
- whether the right in relation to matters relating to the child's own person should be stronger than merely expressing an opinion and should indicate greater influence as the child became older and more able to take responsibility; and
- whether the list of specific matters in which the child should be able to express an opinion was unduly restrictive.

As a result of these debates, the paragraph was strengthened and generalised, so that its ultimate form read:

1. States Parties shall *assure* to the child who is capable of forming his or her own views the right to express those views freely in *all* matters affecting the child, the views of the child being given *due weight* in accordance with the *age and maturity* of the child. [Emphasis added.]

The second paragraph of Article 12 was first proposed by the USA in 1980 as a second paragraph to Article 3. It stated that:

In all judicial or administrative proceedings affecting a child that has reached the age of reason, an opportunity for the views of the child to be heard as an independent party to the proceedings shall be provided, and those views shall be taken into consideration by the competent authorities.[17]

After discussion, the reference to being heard as an independent party was replaced by a reference to 'in a manner consistent with the procedures followed in the State Party for the application of its legislation'. The wording was amended again to facilitate international legal assistance where that was appropriate, so that the final wording read:

2. For this purpose, the child shall in particular be provided the opportunity to be heard in any judicial and administrative proceedings affecting the child, either directly, or through a representative or an appropriate body, in a manner consistent with the procedural rules of national law.

2.3.3 *The Relationship between Views and Interests*

The fact that there was a debate about where to place the provision that ultimately became Article 12.2 indicates the close relationship between the interests and views of children. The initial formulation, which placed it in the context of Article 3, reflected an understanding that ascertainment of the views of the child concerned was an integral part of assessment of interests.

The relationship between Article 12 and Article 3 was further indicated by a statement by one representative that some consideration would have to be given to 'the need to discover the best interests of children not yet capable of forming their own views'.[18] The fact that the problem was identified solely in relation to those children unable to form their own views underlines the importance attached to the views of children in reaching an assessment of their interests.

It is clear that the drafters of the Convention regarded the ascertainment of views as a critical component in assessment of interests. Article 12 impinges on Article 3. The question arises whether this is a one-way or a two-way flow. Does Article 3 also impinge upon Article 12? Is the child's right to express views an absolute right? Are there circumstances in which requiring, encouraging or even inviting the participation of children could act against their interests?

There does not appear to have been a discussion on Article 3 as a qualifier of Article 12. In January 1988 a technical review of the draft convention was authorised. This had several aims. As well as checking the compliance of the draft with other international instruments, the review aimed to:

- identify overlap and repetition between and within the draft articles; and
- check for consistency in the text, including the use of key terms and the use of gender-neutral language, and between the different language versions.

The review did not address or even identify any tension between Articles 3 and 12.

The question of whether concerns about the interests of children should qualify other rights did arise in relation to other articles of the Convention. In relation to freedom of expression, an amendment put forward by the German Democratic Republic to Article 7a (ultimately 13) proposed adding a restriction:

14

> (b) for the protection of national security or of public order [*ordre public*], or of public health or morals, *or the spiritual and moral well-being of the child*;[19]

The USA objected to this additional restriction on freedom of expression on the basis that it would be unfair to impose it on children alone. Such a restriction could be used as an excuse to curtail this right. The paternalistic flavour of the amendment was denounced by one delegate as being 'against the spirit of the Convention.'

The amendment was withdrawn after a debate. Many members felt that the point sought to be addressed by it was already adequately covered by other provisions, for example, the parents' right to guide the child, and therefore no further restriction was justified.

The issue was also debated in the context of freedom of association and freedom of assembly.[20] In an amendment put forward to new Article 7 *ter* (ultimately Article 15) it was proposed that there be further qualifications of the right referring to 'promotion of the best interests of the child'. This was attacked on the basis that it was incompatible with other international obligations[21] and because:

> It was based on the assumption that the child was acting against its best interests, while he was only exercising his rights.

Compromise proposals were put forward, aiming, for example, to impose a restriction:

> where the exercise of these rights would be (manifestly) contrary to the best interests of the child.

It was argued that children could act contrary to their interests, particularly in the case of children without adequate maturity. However, these qualifications were ultimately rejected. The final formulation of Article 15 states that:

1. States Parties recognise the rights of the child to freedom of association and freedom of peaceful assembly.
2. No restrictions may be placed on the exercise of these rights other than those imposed in conformity with the law and which are necessary in a democratic society in the interests of national security or public safety, public order [*ordre public*], the protection of public health or morals or the protection of the rights and freedoms of others.

2.3.4   Conclusion

Nowhere within the text of the Convention or the surrounding debates does Article 3 surface as an implicit qualifier to Article 12. Where concerns about interests arose in the context of other articles, the drafters refused to dilute those articles with reference to the overriding need to protect the interests of the child. Attempts to do so were seen as paternalistic and opening the door to a creeping abrogation of the rights of the child under the Convention.

The following section looks at areas of tension between articles 3 and 12 highlighted in the states parties' reports to the UN Committee on the Rights of the Child, the reports of their meetings with the Committee, and the Committee's response to them.

2.4   The UN Committee on the Rights of the Child

How did the UN Committee respond to attempts by states to implement the Convention? In the course of their consideration of states' reports, issues were sometimes raised about the meaning of Article 12 and its relationship with the best interests of the child. Almost without exception, the Committee commented that further measures were required to achieve full implementation of Article 12. It admitted to expecting higher standards of developed countries[22] but, even in states suffering famine, war and economic disaster, the committee continued to hold that Article 12 set out a basic principle which had to be respected.[23]

The following represent some specific comments on aspects of Article 12 and its relationship to the interests of the child, which were raised in the course of the Committee's considerations.

2.4.1   Belgium

Children under 15 years of age are not allowed to testify on oath in civil or criminal proceedings, although statements can be heard for the purpose of information. There is a further ban on children being heard at all:

> in a case in which his ascendants have opposing interests... a judge in an ordinary court cannot hear testimony, in the context of the examination of witnesses, from the child of two parents who are in conflict over the exercise of parental authority.[24]

There is no bar on hearing the child of only one of the parties, for example, the child of a previous or subsequent relationship. The rationale for the bar on hearing children of the parties in dispute would appear to be a protective one.

Belgium's Initial Report indicated that, whilst this was the current position, legislative amendments under consideration would give children the right to be heard. Moreover, as the Convention is automatically incorporated into the law of Belgium, judicial decisions had already begun to anticipate the formal change which legislation would achieve.

The Belgian delegation was questioned by the Committee on this matter. The Committee's Concluding Observations,[25] encouraged the delegation to proceed with its proposals to facilitate the involvement of children in judicial proceedings and to drop the barriers to participation of children as witnesses.

2.4.2 Canada

In their report to the Committee,[26] the Canadian Government indicated that family law was the area of priority for implementation of Article 12. Implementation in other areas of the law was expected to be gradual.

Concern was expressed about the application of Article 12, even within the area of family law:

> In the area of family law, increased participation of children in custody proceedings, and in particular the matter of independent legal representation of children in court, raise a number of concerns... about a child's ability to instruct counsel and possible damaging effects of asking a child to choose between parents.

Custody proceedings can be taken in respect of children under 16, and older children affected by illness or disability. Canada's comments upon the present position with regard to hearing the views of the child indicate a diverse, pragmatic approach, rather than a consistent, principled one:

> 'The Divorce Act does not specifically provide children with the right to express their views in custody proceedings. However as a matter of practise children's views are often expressed through the evidence of a social worker, psychologist or psychiatrist. A meeting between the child and the judge in chambers may take place. Some provincial jurisdictions provide for legal counsel to represent children in court by way of a guardian *ad litem* or an *amicus curiae*.'

In its Concluding Observations on the Canadian report, the Committee said:

> With regard to article 12 in particular, it is recommended that children be provided with the opportunity to be heard in judicial and administrative proceedings.[27]

2.4.3   France

The French report to the UN Committee indicates that serious thought had been given to the implementation of Article 12, to possible public concern about it, to the central significance of the attitudes of mind of those charged with respecting and implementing the rights guaranteed by the Convention, and to the relationship between the views and interests of the child. The report's opening statement commences:

> Transcending the recognition of the right to protection, the Convention stresses the promotion of the rights of the child... This development is part of an ongoing quest for a balance between an awareness of the aspirations of minors, their protection and parental responsibility in respect of education.[28]

In its discussion of Article 3 – dealing with the best interests of the child – the report acknowledges the importance of the child's views in assessing where his or her interests lie:

> The recognition by the convention of the minor's right of expression undoubtedly gives a new dimension to the concept since, while not making the child the judge of his own interest, it does enable the court to seek further clarifications from the minor to determine where his interest lies.[29]

The report emphasises the distinction between participation and autonomy on the part of a child:

> The fears raised by this article [12] have served to justify drawing the attention of parents and educators to language and practices that are contrary to the child's interests. A consensus has been established on the following ideas: expressing a point of view is not the same thing as taking a decision. Respecting the child's opinions means listening to them, but not necessarily endorsing them. The adult decision-maker's task is to add the child's viewpoint to other elements which might contribute to an enlightened decision. The child's age and maturity are, of course, decisive parameters.[30]

An Act of 8 January 1993 relating to civil status, the family and the rights of the child establishes the post of judge for family affairs and aims to incorporate the principle of Article 12. Children who are capable of forming their own views are entitled to be heard in any proceedings affecting them. This is reported as effectively establishing a new right for the child – the right to speak in proceedings. If a child is emancipated (which is possible from the age of 16) this right is unqualified. With regard to other children, it is possible for a court to refuse a minor's request for a hearing, but it must give a specially reasoned decision for the refusal.[31]

This would appear to be a protective measure. In his opening comments to the Committee, a French delegate, referring to the 1993 law, noted that:

> This law ... extends the child's right to speak in proceedings. Nevertheless, this right, which the law establishes regarding a child capable of discernment, is exercised with strict respect for rules aimed at avoiding the unintended effect of destabilising even more a child who already finds himself in a difficult position. So, if it is anticipated that the interests of the child are going to diverge from those of the parents, the designation of an ad hoc administrator to represent him in these proceedings helps to avoid awkward situations.[32]

The implication of this is that, whilst the basic principle under French law is that the child has a right to be heard directly, by speaking at the proceedings, this right might be curtailed if the court is of the opinion that it would be against the child's interests to do so. In this case, the child's views might be communicated by a representative.

In its Concluding Observations, the Committee welcomed the measures taken by France: 'to recognise the right of the child to have his or her views heard and taken into account in proceedings affecting the child'.[33]

The Committee's suggestions about further measures aimed at implementing Article 12 focused mainly on decision-making processes in the school and the local community.

2.4.4 Norway

Norway's Initial Report to the UN Committee states that:

> Safeguarding what is best for the child, showing consideration for the best interests of the child and respecting the views of children are all part of public policy in Norway, and provisions to this effect are found in several acts.[34]

The Children's Act of 1981 obliges parents to hear the child's opinion before making decisions on personal matters affecting the child. As children get older, parents must give them increasingly greater rights to make their own decisions. Children aged 12 and over have the right to state their opinion before such decisions are made. This includes the choice of parent with whom the child is to live. Considerable weight must be given to the child's wishes.[35]

The obligation to take account of the child's opinion would apply to the divorce or separation of parents. Mediation on matters of custody and access is compulsory before a case comes to court. The report states that:

> It is regarded as important to protect children from their parents' conflicts and to try, whenever possible, to resolve such conflicts by means of a settlement.[36]

Diversion from formal processes is therefore seen in itself as a protective measure. Nor is this informal agreement subject to judicial ratification. The report states that:

> It is assumed that an out-of-court agreement between the parents is usually the best solution for a child.[37]

The presumption is that Article 3 is best served by informal agreements between parents that protect the child from the damaging effect of exposure to their conflict. This protective approach is balanced by the parents' general duty to take the views of the child increasingly into account.

When more formal decisions must be made concerning parental responsibility, daily care and visitation rights, they are made on the basis of the best interests of the child. The child's opinion must be taken into consideration.[38]

Despite these provisions, some concern is expressed by the Committee that there remains an attitude that children's rights are governed by parental discretion. Article 5 of the Convention obliges states to respect the responsibilities and rights of parents:

> to provide, in a manner consistent with the evolving capacities of the child, appropriate direction and guidance in the exercise by the child of the rights recognised in the present Convention.

The Committee minutes report the view of a member of the Committee:

> 'On the question of parental guidance, she had had the impression from the delegation's replies that they regarded article 5 of the convention as applicable only from the parents' point of view. In fact the provision emphasised the need for guidance to take into account the evolving capacities of the child including the exercise of his rights. The exercise of a child's rights with parental guidance had not been fully developed in the report and further information on that aspect would be useful.[39]

The fear was that this approach could lead to a situation in which the parental view of the child's – or even their own – interests could override respect for the child's rights.

Greater appreciation of the right of the child to participate is found in the general rules of civil procedure. If a child under 10 is called to give evidence, the court decides:

> 'based on a careful assessment between consideration for the witness and the value of information to the case, whether such a statement should be taken (cf. S 210, Civil Procedure Act, 13 August 1915 No. 6). If a child is called as a witness and there are reasons to exempt the child in question from the duty to testify, due, for example, to kinship with one of the parties, the main rule is that the child himself (not the guardian) decides whether he wishes to give a statement.[40]

This is an important principle, balancing concern for the welfare of the child with acknowledgement of the child's right to participate.

2.4.5   Poland

Whilst the impetus for the Convention came initially from Poland, its initial draft convention, as already noted, focused on protective rather than participatory rights. When Poland ratified the Convention, a declaration was submitted which had the effect of modifying the application of Articles 12 to 16, that is, those articles relating to rights of participation, freedom of expression, freedom of thought, conscience and religion, freedom of association and the right to protection of privacy. The declaration stated that: 'Exercise by the child of his/her rights should respect the parental authority, in accordance with Polish customs and traditions.'.[41] When questioned by the Committee on the freedom of children to hold and express opinions of their own, the Polish delegation argued that it was a complex issue. To secure a fundamental change in attitude would be a long and difficult process. The report records the explanation that:

> The traditional model of the family, which was the norm in rural areas, was strongly parent–oriented. Under that system, some human rights of the child tended to be neglected. On the other hand, it had to be said that that model assigned the utmost importance to what might be termed the child's 'social' rights, with parents making considerable sacrifices to ensure their children's material welfare.[42]

The delegates acknowledged the need to promote awareness that change was necessary, but estimated that it might take a generation to bring about that change. Accession to the Convention was accelerating that process.

The protective approach was also evident in relation to the child's participation in court proceedings. Whilst 18 is the general age of majority, there is a limited legal capacity from the age of 13. At that age children may be a party in certain types of family or guardianship cases which concern them. Even then: 'the court may limit or exclude the child's personal participation in such proceedings...when educational reasons justify such a decision [art. 573, para. 2, of the Code of Civil Procedure].'[43]

In addition, whilst there is no specific age for giving testimony in civil or criminal proceedings, there is a specific limitation in the case of divorce, nullification of marriage or deciding on the existence or non-existence of a marriage. In these cases, minors under 13 years of age, and descendants of parties under 17 years of age, are specifically prohibited from giving testimony.

This protective exception is replicated in other specific areas. Thus while the consent of 13-year-olds is normally required in adoption, the Family and Guardianship Code sets out an exception:

> In exceptional circumstances the court may waive the demand for such consent if the circumstances prove that the minor considers himself/herself to be the foster parent's child and demand of such consent would be contrary to the minor's interest.

Thus it would be possible under Polish law for a young person of 13 years or more to be adopted without even being aware that it was happening.

In commenting on the Polish approach to the rights of children, a member of the Committee made statements which in part echoed comments referred to above regarding Norway's approach to Article 5:

> Polish legislation rightly spoke of the well-being of the child, but the question seemed to be viewed only from the economic and social angle. She was not sure that the feelings and wishes of children themselves were always taken into account. Furthermore, the provisions of the Family and Guardianship Code concerning the rights and duties of parents were not fully consistent with article 5 of the Convention. The Code seemed to place the emphasis on the rights of parents to provide guidance to their children in exercising their rights. In fact, the emphasis should be on the actual exercise of the rights by the children [...] the provision of Polish law concerning 'inadvisability for educational reasons' might lead to subjective interpretations by the courts that would result in a failure to take the views of the child fully into account.

In its concluding observations, the Committee said it was:

> concerned that traditional attitudes still prevailing in the country may not be conducive to the realisation of the general principles of the Convention,

including in particular article 2 (principle of non-discrimination), article 3 (principle of the best interests of the child), and article 12 (respect for the views of the child).[44]

Whilst acknowledging that changing traditional attitudes did take time, Poland was exhorted to consider removing the declarations relating to Articles 12 to 16 as an indication of its will to do so.[45]

Legal reform was recommended to ensure full conformity with the Convention's principles, including respect for the views of the child.[46]

2.4.6 Russian Federation

The Russian report indicates that the Code on Marriage and the Family ensures that the child's opinion is taken into account in matters concerning paternity, change of name and adoption, if the child is aged 10 or over.[47] Further legislation is planned to facilitate participation by children in judicial, administrative and other proceedings. The report indicates that:

> The federal Bill on the protection of the family, mothers, fathers and children, contains a provision whereby a child will have the right to be heard during judicial, administrative and other proceedings if by virtue of its level of development, it is able to comprehend what is happening and to express its own views freely. The child's opinion must be taken into account when the court takes its decision.[48]

The interest of the Russian report lies in the fact that it represents one of the few occasions when a question was put directly about how to balance respect for the child's views with a focus on their interests.

In response to a question by the Committee concerning participation, the Russian delegates acknowledged that:

> There were no directly relevant standard setting instruments, but the desirability of a child's participation in proceedings was assessed in special cases, in the light of the child's interests. For example, recommendations existed concerning adoption, to the effect that discussions should be held with both the child and the adoptive parents concerning issues affecting the child.[49]

With regard to adoption, a member of the committee asked:

how the government of the Russian Federation reconciled the principle of respect for the best interests of the child with the right of children to express their opinions about their adoption..[50]

The delegation replied that:

> The child's opinion was taken into account when adoption was envisaged. If a child did not wish to join a given family he was interviewed, and the adoption did not take place if he did not wish it.[51]

2.4.7 Sweden

The Code of Parenthood and Guardianship addresses custody, access and maintenance issues and applies up to the age of 18. This states that:

> It is the right and duty of the custodian to decide matters relating to the child's personal affairs. In doing so, and in step with the child's advancing age and development, the custodian shall make increasing allowance for the child's views and wishes.[52]

Questions of custody and access have been regulated by statute law on the assumption that, as a rule, the best thing for the child is for the parents to be able to agree on these matters.[53] If the matter does come to court, children may testify if there are special grounds why they should do so and it is obvious that they will not suffer harm as a result. It is also possible for the court to order an investigation of the custody and access issues, in which case the child's opinion is also obtained 'by suitable means'.[54]

Thus, whereas France (see above) requires a stated reason for refusal to allow a child to speak in proceedings, Sweden requires a case to be made to justify the child speaking. In both countries the child may be refused a hearing on the grounds that it would not be in the child's interests. However, the starting point is quite different.

On the other hand, Sweden seems to go further with regard to the implementation of court orders. If the child has reached the age of 12, a custody or access decision may not be put into effect against the child's wishes, except where the court finds this necessary in the child's best interests. The same applies if a child is not yet 12 years old but has attained such a degree of maturity that his or her wishes should be similarly taken into account.[55]

This makes the child's views the starting point as regards implementation of such orders.

In the area of child welfare, covered by the Social Services Act and the Care of Young Persons (Special Measures) Act, the law operates on the principle that measures taken by social services for children and young persons must in the first instance be based on consensus with the parents (custodians) and with the child him- or herself if he or she is 15 or over.

Young people of 15 years or more can conduct their own cases and are entitled to speak on their own behalf in judicial and administrative proceedings affecting them. Under-15s should be given a hearing 'if there is no presumption that it will be harmful to them'. Children are entitled to legal counsel.[56]

The report indicates that Sweden has taken a considered approach to the question of child witnesses in all legal fora:

> There is no formal objection to children testifying in court, but because this can have serious personal consequences for the child, it has been left to the courts to decide, in the case of children under 15, whether or not they should be called upon to testify. Great importance is attached to the parent or custodian's opinion in this matter. Sometimes it may also be appropriate to consult a medical practitioner on the subject. The usual arrangement is for the child not to be questioned in court but to give evidence, for example in a statement to the police or in the course of custody and access investigations. The statement is video-recorded or phonetically transcribed. Conversations taking place with children in the course of custody investigations are usually presented in writing. A person under 15, however, cannot testify on oath, nor can he incur any sanctions (contingent fines or remand in custody) for refusing to testify. On the other hand, a child can be forcibly conveyed to court.[57]

An issue of concern to the Committee was the right of Swedish children to legal and medical counselling irrespective of their age and without parental consent. This was facilitated by the fact that medical counselling was available at school or in special social and medical advice centres for young people. In practice, children from the age of seven could obtain medical advice without parental consent through access to the school doctor or nurse. [58]

In the course of the Committee proceedings, a member commented that: 'The Swedish Government might also wish to further consider the advisability of permitting a child of seven years or older to accept legal or medical counselling without parental consent.'[59] The Concluding Observations contained a recommendation that: 'The Government may also wish to reassess the advisability of permitting a child of seven years or older to accept legal or medical counselling without parental consent.'[60]

Some interesting general debates took place concerning the balance between the views and interests of children. A member of the Committee commented:

> On the question of the best interests of the child ... it was possible for children to form mistaken opinions owing to their immaturity and inexperience, so that a contradiction might arise between their best interests and respect for their views. He would like to know what Sweden thought of that problem.[61]

The delegation responded that the question was an extremely complex one which it was difficult to answer well. Rather than give a direct answer, delegates responded on the basis that ascertainment of a child's views was an essential part of determining his or her best interests. They said that:

> As children grew up their opinions and wishes were increasingly taken into consideration, and from the age of 18 they had every right to control their own lives even when that was not objectively in their best interests. It was important to try to establish dialogue with children and together find out their best interests. That was not something that could be resolved through legislation.[62]

An interesting exchange took place on the issue of what constituted 'a child's perspective'. A member of the Committee referred to a reference in the report to attempts to develop a child's perspective in the activities of the social services. It had been stated that methods of investigation and documentation were being explored from the child's perspective. However, the report had also said that a child's perspective was not always considered to be coincident with the principle of due weight being given to the child's opinion. How was that reflected in practice and what could other countries learn from it?[63]

The delegates responded that developing a child's perspective meant not only looking at situations through the child's eyes, but having knowledge of his or her needs and level of development. To that end, the National Board of Health and Welfare had been commissioned to study the matter further.[64]

A question was also asked about whether Swedish children were not 'over-protected'. The response was that there was strong protection but also many bodies funded to represent young people.[65]

A member of the Committee concluded that:

> It was important for Sweden to reconcile the need for social protection of children with respect for their rights to privacy and individual choice.[66]

It was noted by the Committee that:

> while there were still some outstanding issues which might be improved, Sweden must generally be regarded as a country which looked upon children favourably. At the same time, it must be recognised that the greater the possibilities and achievements of a state, the more demanding its society became. Moreover, the international community inevitably tended to evaluate the status of children in what it considered to be 'model' states, of which in many respects Sweden was one. It was important, therefore, to avoid any devaluation of the State's current high standard of protection of children.[67]

2.4.8 UK

The concluding observations of the UN Committee with regard to the UK noted that the Government's initial report[68] had:

> lacked sufficient information on the factors and difficulties impeding the implementation of various rights provided for in the Convention.[69]

The report had focused attention on the changes introduced by the Children Act 1989 for England and Wales, and forthcoming legislation for Scotland and Northern Ireland. The Committee noted the changes made by the 1989 Act, but expressed its concern about:

> the apparent insufficiency of measures taken to ensure the implementation of the general principles of the Convention, namely the provisions of its articles 2, 3, 6 and 12.[70]

There was debate in the Committee about the meaning of Article 12.1. The Committee indicated their perception that, in its replies to their questions, the UK seemed to suggest that consulting the child on his or her views was seen as a matter of discretion rather than a right. Whereas the Committee's view was that:

> The terms of article 12, para. 1, however, clearly set out the child's right to express his views in matters affecting his own life.[71]

The Committee was particularly concerned about the lack of respect for Article 12 in the education field. In England and Wales, parents had a right to withdraw their children from parts of the sex education programmes in schools. Throughout the UK, children were not entitled to express their opinion when they were excluded from school.

The Committee's recommendations included greater respect for Article 12 in law, policy and practice. They made, in addition, a specific recommendation relating to children's rights within the education system.

In general, the Committee seemed to consider that the UK was complacent about its compliance with the Convention and required to take a more critical look at the actual state of children's rights. A mechanism for co-ordinating and monitoring implementation of the Convention was recommended as an important step towards achieving full compliance.

2.5   Assessment of the Committee's Responses

Belgium was encouraged to proceed with plans to facilitate participation of children in legal proceedings, in a move away from a very protective stance which had formed a barrier to participation.

Canada presented a protective approach towards participation of children and was advised to allow greater opportunity for children to be heard in judicial and administrative proceedings.

The French report took the most thoughtful approach, clearly rooted in the principles of the Convention. It did acknowledge that, in exceptional cases, the child's right to have his or her interests respected might create a situation in which a request to be heard directly might be refused. However, a representative would be appointed for the child, whose views would be transmitted by more indirect means. The Committee offered no adverse comment on this approach.

In Norway, formal processes gave the child a degree of involvement and control over whether to testify. However, informal, diversionary processes aimed at protecting the child took less account of the child's views. The Committee felt that Norway placed too much emphasis on the parent's right to guide the child, at the expense of the child's right to participate. This imbalance required to be redressed.

Poland's recourse to traditional attitudes as a justification for delaying implementation of Article 12 was not accepted. The Committee felt there was no excuse for Poland's declaration aimed at modifying application of the Article. This showed a lack of commitment. Moreover, the protective approach to participation of children in proceedings opened the door to subjective interpretations which gave little weight to the actual wishes and feelings of the child.

The reports relating to Sweden and the Russian Federation are evidence of some discussion on the issue of the influence of Article 3 on Article 12. The Swedish papers are of interest because of the ambivalence of the Committee's response. Whilst overall commending Sweden for its high standards in relation to the protection of children, the Committee asked whether Sweden was not too protective. At the same time, the Committee sounded a cautionary note about the freedom of Swedish children to seek legal and medical advice from about the age of seven without parental consent. It seems clear that the Committee thought this was too young an age for these activities.

In its response to the UK report, the Committee again made it clear that the rights of children under the Convention were truly rights adhering to them as individuals, and not to be dispensed at the discretion of governments or parents.

The conclusion from the above must be that the Committee views Article 12 as free-standing and unqualified. The child's right to express views and have them taken into account is one of the basic principles of the Convention; it is not to be set aside because of government reluctance or parental concern. Whilst that concern may be real, and justified in the context of procedures inimical to participation by children, the correct response is to change the system and the procedures to accommodate children. That is a challenge which must be taken up by governments.

As for parents, their right to provide guidance to the child is fully supported by the Convention and by the Committee, but the Committee repeatedly emphasised that the right is to provide appropriate direction and guidance; not to direct that the child's rights shall not be observed. The Committee's concern about the low age for independent access to legal and medical counselling in Sweden is an indication of the value placed on *appropriate* parental direction and guidance.

The Committee appeared to favour the French approach of assuming a right to be heard directly, if that is what the child wants. In the French system, such a request would be refused only on the basis of a reasoned decision, and an alternative participation mechanism substituted.

Children who are capable of forming views have a right to participate in decisions regarding all matters affecting them. The above analysis justifies a conclusion that that right is an absolute one, although the interests of children may be relevant in determining the mode in which it is to be exercised.

Notes

1. General Assembly of the United Nations (1989), *The Convention on the Rights of the Child*.
2. Detrick (1991)., p. 641.
3. Ibid.
4. Ibid., p. 19.
5. United Nations Declaration of the Rights of the Child, Principle 2: 'The child shall enjoy special protection, and shall be given opportunities and facilities, by law and by other means, to enable him to develop physically, mentally, morally, spiritually and socially in a healthy and normal manner and in conditions of freedom and dignity. In the enactment of laws for this purpose, the best interests of the child shall be the paramount consideration.'
6. Ibid., Principle 7: 'The best interests of the child shall be the guiding principle of those responsible for his education and guidance; that responsibility lies in the first place with his parents'.
7. Collins English Dictionary (1991), Third Edition.

8. Ibid.
9. Vienna Convention on the Law of Treaties, Article 32, quoted Detrick (1991), p. 113.
10. Detrick, (1991).
11. Ibid., p. 133.
12. Ibid., p. 137.
13. UN paper E/CN.4/1989/WG.1/CRP.1, p. 14.
14. Detrick, (1991), p. 137.
15. Ibid., p. 80.
16. Ibid., p. 81.
17. Ibid., p. 132.
18. Ibid., pp. 134, 225.
19. Detrick (1991), p. 236.
20. Ibid., p. 253.
21. International Covenant on Civil and Political Rights, Article 22, Para. 2.
22. See comments on Sweden in 2.4.7.
23. For example in its concluding observations on Nicaragua, described as 'one of the poorest countries in Latin America', see UN paper CRC/C/15/Add. 36, at Paras 8 and 33.
24. UN paper CRC/C/11/Add. 4.
25. UN paper CRC/C/15/Add. 38.
26. UN paper CRC/11/Add. 3, Para. 81.
27. UN paper CRC/C/15/Add. 37, para. 23.
28. UN paper CRC/C/3/Add. 15, Para.1.
29. Ibid., Para.167.
30. Ibid., Para 183.
31. Ibid., Para. 86.
32. UN paper CRC/C/SR.139, Para.6; author's translation from French original.
33. UN paper CRC/C/29, Para. 85.
34. UN paper CRC/C/8/Add. 7, Para. 166.
35. UN paper CRC/C/8/Add. 7, Para. 63.
36. Ibid., Para. 172.
37. Ibid., Para. 184.
38. Ibid., Para. 94.
39. UN paper CRC/C/SR.150, Para. 42.
40. UN paper CRC/C/8/Add. 7, Para. 76.
41. UN paper CRC/C/8/Add. 11, Para. 81.
42. UN paper CRC/C/SR. 193, Para. 18.
43. UN paper CRC/C/8/Add. 11, Para. 43.
44. UN paper CRC/C/38, Para. 114.
45. Ibid., Para. 123 and CRC/C/SR. 193, Para. 22.
46. UN paper CRC/C/38, Para. 131.
47. UN paper CRC/C/3/Add. 5, Para. 66.
48. Ibid., Para. 67.
49. UN paper CRC/C/SR. 62, Para. 28.
50. UN paper CRC/C/SR. 63, Para. 19.

51. Ibid., Para. 53.
52. UN paper CRC/C/3/Add. 1, Para. 54.
53. Ibid., Para. 91.
54. Ibid., Para. 40.
55. UN paper CRC/C/3/Add. 1, Para. 54.
56. Ibid., Para. 40.
57. Ibid., Para. 13.
58. UN paper CRC/C/SR. 56, Para. 33.
59. UN paper CRC/C/SR. 58, Para. 6.
60. UN paper CRC/C/15/Add. 2, Para 11.
61. UN paper CRC/C/SR. 56, Para. 19.
62. Ibid., Para. 30.
63. Ibid., Para. 25.
64. Ibid., Para. 37.
65. Ibid., Para. 33.
66. UN paper CRC/C/SR.58, Para. 11.
67. UN paper CRC/C/SR.58, Para. 4.
68. (1994) *The UK's First Report to the UN Committee on the Rights of the Child*; London, HMSO.
69. UN paper CRC/C/15 Add. 34, Part A.
70. Ibid., Part C.
71. UN paper CRC/C/SR. 205, Para. 28.

Chapter 3

◆

MODES OF PARTICIPATION

Introduction

It is one thing to state that children have a right to participate in matters affecting them. Putting that principle into practice is a more complex task. It is clearly not sufficient to extend adult processes to children. In Scotland, an attempt to facilitate children's participation by doing this was greeted with dismay (see 4.4.4 'Scotland' below).

The implications of the right to participate extend both to formal and informal decision-making settings. Three levels of formality might be identified:

1. informal decisions within the family;
2. informal processes, such as family mediation services or social work meetings; and
3. formal, judicial processes.

This chapter looks at ways in which their commitment to Article 12 is expressed by those states which chose to go into detail about the matter in their reports to the UN. Fuller information is given about participation mechanisms in Scotland, England and Wales.

3.2   Informal Decisions Within the Family

The least formal would be within the family itself. Some countries, such as Norway and Sweden, have placed on parents a legal obligation to consult their children on matters affecting them.

The Norwegian provision is described in the Initial Report to the UN as follows:

According to section 31 of Act No. 7 of 8 April 1981 relating to children and parents (Children's Act), as the child gradually develops and matures, the parents shall hear the child's opinion before making decisions on personal matters affecting the child. When the child has attained the age of 12, he shall be allowed to state his opinion before decisions are made on personal matters on his behalf, including with which of his parents he wishes to live. Considerable weight shall be given to the child's wishes.[1]

Parents shall give the child increasingly greater rights to make his own decisions as he gets older and until he comes of age. [Cf. Section 33 of the Children's Act.][2]

In Sweden, the Code of Parenthood and Guardianship [Chap. 6, S. 11] states that:

It is the right and duty of the custodian to decide matters relating to the child's personal affairs. In doing so, and in step with the child's advancing age and development, the custodian shall make increasing allowance for the child's views and wishes.[3]

In Denmark, while there is no legal obligation as such, the Initial Report to the UN Committee states that:

It is the generally accepted view that as the child develops and matures, parents should involve the child and attach weight to the child's views when decisions are to be made on personal matters relating to the child.[4]

In Scotland, a new Act operative from 1 November 1996 provides that:

A person shall, in reaching any major decision which involves –
   (a) his fulfilling a parental responsibility …;or
   (b) his exercising a parental right …,

have regard so far as practicable to the views (if he wishes to express them) of the child concerned, taking account of the child's age and maturity …; and without prejudice to the generality of this subsection a child twelve years of age or more shall be presumed to be of sufficient age and maturity to form a view.[5]

Whilst questions have been raised about the enforceability of such provisions, they are regarded as valuable statements of principle which could have some legal implications in individual cases.

3.3   Informal Processes

There are informal processes which might involve children, for example family mediation, or social work meetings outside the judicial process. With regard to family mediation in the UK, involvement of children is increasingly an aspect of policy, although the mode and extent of participation varies amongst services.

Children in care in the UK have, for a number of years, had a statutory right to be consulted on matters affecting them.[6]

In Denmark, the Social Assistance Act operates on the principle that the best way to support the child is to support the parents. In some fields, the opinion of children is prescribed as part of the decision-making process. Children of 12 have the right to be consulted about proposed measures of family assistance. The Initial Report to the UN states that:

> An interview must always be offered, but it is up to the child or young person to decide whether such an interview is to be carried out. In the case of children under the age of 12 years, information on the child's opinion about an intended measure must be made available; however, only to the extent warranted by the maturity of the child and the nature of the case.

The Norwegian Initial Report states that, in child welfare cases:

> the child shall be informed and his advice sought ... when it is reasonable to do so considering his development, maturity and the kind of matter in question. If the child is 12 years or older, he must always be given the opportunity to express an opinion before a decision is made with regard to placing the child in question in a foster home, institution or with regard to a subsequent move. Due consideration shall be paid to the child's opinion.[7]

The Swedish Initial Report notes that:

> Under the Social Services Act, a child must be given the opportunity of speaking on its own behalf in dealings with social services, especially when the question arises of placing the child away from its parental home.[8]

While these provisions are to be welcomed, monitoring is clearly necessary to ensure that they are working effectively. Chapter 5 of this book sets out comments of professionals and young people that are relevant to the reality of the implementation of such rights.

3.4   Formal, Judicial Processes

Some of the initial formulations of the UN Convention contained proposals that children be given the right to be heard as independent parties to the proceedings.[9] In the course of debate, these proposals became less specific and compromise was ultimately reached on the current wording of Article 12.2:

> For this purpose, the child shall in particular be provided the opportunity to be heard in any judicial and administrative proceedings affecting the child, either directly or indirectly, or through a representative or an appropriate body, in a manner consistent with the procedural rules of national law.

The issue was also discussed in the context of proceedings involving abused or neglected children. In the debate surrounding Article 8 bis, which ultimately became Article 19, the USA proposed that states be required to:

> (h) provide for the appointment of a legal representative to represent the legal interests of the child in judicial proceedings involving an abused or neglected child.[10]

There was some criticism of the fuller USA proposal, of which this was a part, on the grounds that it focused too much on judicial procedures. The eventual form of Article 19 made a general reference to appropriate judicial involvement, but contained no specific requirements on the representation of children's interests.

Apart from this specific provision in Article 19, what we find in the Convention is:

- in relation to the child's views, a requirement in Article 12 that the child be heard, 'either directly or indirectly, or through a representative or an appropriate body'; and
- in relation to the child's interests, a general principle in Article 3 about establishing interests as a criterion for decision-making, with no direction as to how this aim is to be achieved.

The lack of specification with regard to Article 3 is not surprising given the variety of approaches in different legal systems, and even in different areas of the same legal system. A process whose basic aim is pursuit of the child's interest and which operates an inquisitorial system will require a different mechanism than an adversarial process aiming to resolve differences between competing adult parties, where the child is in the middle.

States report a variety of approaches to participation by children in formal, legal processes. They generally have different provisions for cases involving private law and public law. Private law involves issues relating to children within their own families (for example, matters of residence and contact when parents split up). Public law concerns children involved with social services, when the parents' ability to care for the children is in question.

There is also a diversity of approach to representation of the views and interests of children. Whilst views and interests are frequently referred to in the reports which follow, it will be clear that the remit of a child representative or advocate is not always clearly defined, nor the tensions inherent in a dual role adequately identified.

3.4.1   Canada

As discussed in 2.4.2 above, Canada's approach is diverse and pragmatic rather than principled. Some variety of approach is found amongst the provinces and territories of Canada.

In Alberta, the courts have established a principle that, in legal matters affecting children, those aged 12 and over are capable of giving 'reasoned views' and ought to be consulted. Their opinions are to be given considerable weight. In most cases, the child's guardian would provide representation for the child and ensure that his or her views were expressed. Whereas, where children were receiving protective services from the state, the Children's Advocate would have the responsibility of ensuring that the child's right to be heard was respected.

This office was set up by the Child Welfare Amendment Act 1988. The Advocate is mandated to represent the rights, interest and viewpoints of children receiving services under the Child Welfare Act, to investigate complaints with respect to the provision of child welfare services, and to provide advice and recommendations to the Minister with respect to Alberta's child welfare system. The Children's Advocate can only intervene if invited by the child to advocate on his or her behalf.

In Ontario private custody disputes are regulated by the Children's Law Reform Act which provides that the courts shall consider 'the views and preferences of the child, where such views and preferences reasonably can be ascertained'. In civil proceedings involving a minor, there must be a litigation guardian who is to act in the best interests of the minor (Rule of Civil Procedure). There is an Official Guardian located in the Ministry of the Attorney General, whose duty it is to 'represent the legal interests of children'. He or she provides free legal representation for minors where the court directs representation in various child-care and protection proceedings, and may be requested to investigate and report to the court on all matters concerning custody and access [Courts of Justice Act].

In child-care proceedings in Ontario, the child is entitled to legal representation at every stage. The right to obtain legal counsel without parental consent is based not on age but on capacity to retain and instruct a lawyer.

In Manitoba, the Child and Family Services Act deals with family support and child protection. The report to the UN states that:

> Children 12 years of age or more are entitled to be advised of any proceedings and are to be given an opportunity to have their views and preferences known. The courts may order that legal counsel be appointed to represent the interests of children 12 years of age or over in a child protection hearing. The courts may also consider the views and preferences of children under 12 years of age. [11]

Manitoba also has a Children's Advocate whose role is to review and investigate complaints relating to children receiving or entitled to receive services and to the services provided. The goals of the Children's Advocate are to:

1. ensure that children have the right and opportunity to communicate their feelings, preferences and opinions;
2. assist children by representing their rights, viewpoints and interest; and
3. identify systemic issues.[12]

Newfoundland's Child Welfare Act states that the court can consult the child regarding what order to make:

> In determining the best interests of the child the court shall consider the views and preferences of the child where those views and preferences can be reasonably ascertained. As a matter of policy a child can have his or her own legal counsel appointed if their views are different from those of the department.[13]

Within this diversity in Canada, whilst reference is made to the expression of views, the role of the representative or advocate is generally not clearly defined. Sometimes it is stated to be the representation of the child's interests, with regard to the child's views. In Ontario's child-care proceedings and Newfoundland's Child Welfare Act there are indications that counsel might actually represent the views of the child.

3.4.2 France

In France there is recognition of the need for those subject to legal incapacity to have a mechanism for bringing their concerns before the judicial authorities.

> At any age a child may bring a matter before a juvenile magistrate and request the assistance of a lawyer. If the minor is 16 years of age or older, the juvenile magistrate must notify him of his decisions and the minor can appeal against those decisions. When the child reaches the age of discernment, he may be heard or request to be heard in any proceedings that concern him.[14]

The child may be heard alone, with a person of his choice, or a lawyer and may in the latter case have the benefit of legal aid. In the course of the UN Committee's consideration of France's Initial Report, the French delegation was at pains to point out that the child had a right to be heard with the assistance of a lawyer in all legal proceedings.[15]

The right to be heard is distinguished from the right to be party to the proceedings, which is not granted by the Act. It is also distinguished from the right of the child to representation of his or her distinct interests. The report indicates that:

when the interests of the child are involved in the proceedings, but differ from those of his parents, the Act of 8 Jan 1993 facilitates the appointment of an ad hoc administrator to represent him in the proceedings, designated ex officio, by the judge, or at the request of the minor himself.[16]

It would appear that there is recognition in France of the different roles with regard to views and interests that a representative might play, and the relationship of these to the additional possibility of the child being a party to the proceedings.

3.4.3 *Norway*

Norway's report to the UN Committee distinguishes between civil cases, child welfare cases, and cases involving 'the public administration'.

A child may be party to a civil case. The Civil Procedure Act provides that civil actions against or on behalf of minors are to be filed against or by the guardian. Children older than 16 years must be summoned to court hearings and receive copies of the written pleadings at the same time as the guardian.[17]

Although minors may not normally conduct legal proceedings themselves they may testify as a party to the case at the request of the court or the parties' legal representatives.[18]

Decisions under the Child Welfare Act are made by an independent public county social welfare board, which is subject to judicial review. Children can claim party rights from the age of 15 if they understand what the case involves. Under-15s can get party rights in special cases. They are always a party, regardless of age, if the case concerns measures for children with behavioural problems.[19]

Being a party to child welfare proceedings means that there are no restrictions on the right to be present during the oral negotiations which must be heard in cases that are to be brought before the county social welfare board.[20] Children who have party rights may also demand a legal review of the board's decision.[21] Parties usually have the right to inspect case documents, and the right to be represented by a lawyer or other representative in all phases of the proceedings.[22]

In cases decided by the public administration, the minor is also represented by the guardian, or a representative appointed by the guardian. Minors thus have the right to be notified through their representatives and to express views in the same way as other parties. Minors over 14 years of age must also be notified directly and be given the opportunity to express their views themselves (see Section 16 of the Public Administration Act).[23]

Children thus appear to have different rights at different ages according to the nature of the proceedings in which they are involved. When they have 'party rights' this does not necessarily mean that they are directly involved in the proceedings, which may be conducted by their guardians. On the other hand, parties to child welfare proceedings, including children, have the right to be present during the oral negotiations, and a right to inspect documents, although it is indicated that there may be some exceptions to this.

3.4.4   UK

Whilst not a federal country like Canada or the USA, the UK has different legal jurisdictions within it. England and Wales form one jurisdiction; Northern Ireland is separate but with laws based upon and similar to those of England and Wales; Scotland has a distinctive legal system with quite different historical roots and concepts.

England and Wales

The main piece of legislation for England and Wales is the Children Act 1989.[24] Whilst the Act addresses issues in private and public law, the approach to the participation of children and representation of their views and interests is different in the two spheres.

The UK Government explained the issue of representation in its Initial Report to the UN Committee on the Rights of the Child. With regard to Article 3, concerning the interests of the child, it stated that:

> In many private law proceedings a court welfare officer will be appointed. He will report to the court on what is in the child's best interests ...
>
> In public law proceedings the courts are required to appoint a guardian ad litem for the child unless satisfied that it is not necessary to do so in

order to safeguard his interests. The guardian is under a duty to safeguard the child's interests.[25]

With regard to Article 12 – the views of the child – the report stated that:

> A central feature of the Children Act, which applies in England and Wales is that the voice of the child must be heard. When a court determines a question about the upbringing of a child they have to have regard in particular to the ascertainable wishes and feelings of the child. The Act allows children for the first time, if they obtain the leave of the court, to apply in their own right for certain orders.
>
> In many private law proceedings a court welfare officer or the Official Solicitor will be appointed. One of his duties is to ascertain the wishes and feelings of the child and convey these to the court.
>
> In most public law proceedings a guardian ad litem will be appointed for the child. One of the guardian's specific tasks under the Court Rules is to report to the court on the wishes of the child in respect of matters relating to the proceedings. If the child is capable of instructing his solicitor direct he may do so separately from the guardian.

While it is envisaged that presentation of the child's views will be a part of the remit of those representing the child's interests, it is also possible for children to have their views represented by a solicitor. In private law cases, this will happen only if the child has successfully obtained leave of court to apply for an order. In public law cases, this will happen if the solicitor decides that he or she can take instructions directly from the child instead of through the guardian.

Thus, in public law cases, a child must have a guardian ad litem, and may have his or her own solicitor. In private law cases, a child who obtains leave to apply will have a solicitor. He or she may have the equivalent of a guardian (a 'next friend'), but this is not essential.[26]

In practice, the provisions in England and Wales seem to be regarded more highly in their public law application than in private law. In line with other jurisdictions, there is a greater willingness to facilitate independent representation of children in public law than in private law cases. The general presumption is that parents will normally safeguard the child's rights. It is more difficult to adhere to this presumption in public law cases where it is precisely the parents' ability to fulfil the child's needs that is in question.

The Children Act Advisory Committee was appointed to monitor the implementation of the 1989 Act. In its annual report for 1992/3, it noted that courts were employing a 'device' to get access to the guardians ad litem in private law cases. This seems to have happened partly to obtain representation for the child at public expense, and partly to avoid the delays associated with reports from court welfare officers.[27] The Advisory Committee's 1993–4 report stated that this misuse had since been largely res olved through case law.[28] It also noted that:

> The help and advice the guardian ad litem gives to the courts.....is valued highly at all levels of court ... The impartiality of the GALRO [guardian ad litem – reporting officer] practice in ensuring that the child's welfare remains paramount was confirmed in an inspection of three panels.[29]

Children may have party status in relation to private law or public law proceedings,[30] but this does not mean that the child will necessarily be present. The Advisory Committee's report refers to a case in which a judge, allowing a girl of 13 to be present during an appeal relative to care proceedings, expressed concern about the presence of children in court:

> The judge said that young children should be discouraged from attending court and guardians ad litem should think carefully before arranging for a child to be present during court proceedings, and should be able to give their reasons to the judge.[31]

The report also refers to an unreported case in which a 15 year old girl was not allowed to be present:

> There was an application by a 15-year-old girl to be present in court during the determination of her appeal against a care order made in the family proceedings court. The girl was represented by solicitors and counsel, and the guardian ad litem was separately represented. The girl had been present throughout the proceedings in the family proceedings court. It was argued that the court had no discretion to exclude the girl from the hearing. While it was agreed that she was old enough to give instructions and to understand and follow the proceedings, the judge concluded that she was emotionally disturbed, that anxious concerns about her would inhibit submissions to the court and that the matters under discussion could represent a source of potential emotional damage. She was ordered to

leave the court during the hearing of the appeal and it was said that there would have to be exceptional circumstances for a girl of 15 to be present in court whilst her affairs were being discussed, having regard to the welfare considerations. In giving guidance on the procedure to be followed whenever a child sought to be present in court, the court should be informed in advance of any application, which would be ruled upon by the bench, before the substantive hearing commenced. Such a procedure would prevent the child from being exposed to any distress or harm, and would enable the court to consider representations with the welfare of the child as the paramount consideration.[32]

The matter was further expanded upon in the Advisory Committee's Annual Report for 1993–4:

> Both the Court of Appeal and Family Division Judges have emphasised that very careful consideration should be given to this and, generally speaking, it is only where there is some clear benefit to the child from attending court that it should be permitted. The very nature of the legal process is such that the child's attention may not be fully engaged and consequently he or she might derive little benefit from being present.
>
> The presence of a guardian ad litem on behalf of a child will usually mean that the presence of a child applicant is unnecessary. There may be problems where a child applicant does not have a guardian ad litem and instructs a solicitor direct; however, even here, the presumption should be that the child should not attend. This will be an issue which the court must consider carefully with the assistance of the child's legal advisors.[33]

The report goes on to consider that it might be possible for an older child to be present to hear the court's decision and the reasons for it. However, it says:

> It would clearly be undesirable for the child to hear a critical cross examination of a parent in respect of their deficiencies or medical evidence about their psychological or sexual behaviour.

On the other hand, since the introduction of the Children Act 1989, courts have been more willing than before to interview children in private.[34]

The Advisory Committee noted the UK ratification of the Convention on the Rights of the Child, and expressed the opinion that 'the Children Act meets most of the Convention's provisions and certainly all the main articles'.[35]

The position in England and Wales is therefore that there are mechanisms to facilitate representation of the views and interests of children in legal proceedings, although both aspects are not necessarily separately represented in every case. Whilst those charged with representing interests must take the child's views into account, there is also a possibility of a child instructing a solicitor direct to represent his or her views. In private law cases, this is dependent upon obtaining leave of court. In public law cases, it is dependent upon the solicitor's willingness to take independent instructions from the child.

The child may be party to the proceedings, but there is a strong presumption against attendance of the child at the proceedings. It is felt that presence is more likely than not to be damaging to the child, and that the presence of the child will inhibit others from discussing matters with the openness necessary to facilitate a decision which truly serves the child's best interests.

Scotland

On 1 April 1997 a new piece of legislation came fully into effect in Scotland. The Children (Scotland) Act 1995 is a first attempt to translate into Scottish legislation the principles of the UN Convention. The Act deals with both private and public law relating to children.

The legal framework which preceded the 1995 Act had been struggling to accommodate the rights guaranteed under the Convention. The Children (Scotland) Act has helped by introducing a conceptual framework more sympathetic to the UN Convention, although the mechanisms for translating it into practice are still being developed.

Scottish private law has long regarded the welfare of the child as paramount in cases concerning parental rights.[36] The mechanisms by which those interests are presented to and are safeguarded before the court are, in spite of the new Act, still patchy and lack a principled basis. Under the traditional common law, courts can appoint a curator ad litem, to represent the interests of the child, although this is rarely done. Courts may also appoint a reporter to investigate and report on the arrangements for the child's care and upbring.[37]

Whilst there is an expectation that those representing the interests of children will have regard to their views, there is no clear guidance, or training for those undertaking that task. Those appointed to investigate the interests of children are usually lawyers or social workers. It must be questioned how appropriate some appointments are. What expertise is required to make such an assessment? What are the values on which the assessment is based? If they seek the views of children, how should they do this? How does one communicate such matters to children and elicit their views? These questions have never been specifically addressed.

There was for some time a debate about the legal capacity of children to instruct solicitors and enter proceedings. This has now been clarified by the 1995 Act which says that children have capacity to instruct solicitors and enter legal proceedings where they have a general understanding of what it means to do so.[38]

In July 1993 new rules of court were passed for the sheriff courts in Scotland, coming into effect on 1 January 1994.[39] In an attempt to take account of Article 12 of the UN Convention, the rules introduced a procedure for serving notice on children who were affected by a family action, but were not party to it. Rule 33.7 (1) provided that:

> (1) In the initial writ in a family action, the pursuer shall include a crave for a warrant for intimation –
>
> > (h) in an action which affects a child, to that child if not a party to the action, and a notice of intimation in Form F9 shall be attached to the initial writ intimated to the child.

This well-intentioned move caused considerable anxiety. It was generally felt that the form of intimation would be unintelligible to most children. The papers which accompanied it might include information which it was neither helpful nor appropriate for the child to see. There was a lack of clarity about what legal processes should follow if a child wished to enter the proceedings. In addition, sheriffs were not sure whether they were obliged to intimate the action on the child or whether they had discretion not to. This is said to have resulted in some authorising service upon infants in the pram.

As a result of these concerns, considerable thought was given to the introduction of a more appropriate procedure. Amendments to the Rules of Court in 1996 introduced a revised and simplified Form F9. Both the old and the new forms are set out in Appendix 2 for the purpose of comparison. It is also intended that these forms should be sent out on their own, without the accompanying legal documentation.

In addition, the amended Rules allow for the possibility of the child's views being recorded in writing and placed in a sealed envelope accessible only to the Sheriff.[40]

Clearly it would be helpful to have an evaluation in due course of the impact of these changes.

In public law cases, the Scottish situation is quite different from that in the rest of the UK. An innovative Act of 1968 (The Social Work (Scotland) Act) had established Scotland's unique children's hearing system. The 1995 Act retained the children's hearing system as the central organ of compulsory child care and protection in Scotland.

The system was based on proposals by the Kilbrandon Commission[41] which was set up largely to look at mechanisms for dealing with young offenders. The Commission proceeded on the basis that offending behaviour by a child was only one of a number of indicators of a need for care. The children's hearing system which was set up as a result, made no distinction between offenders and others.

At a hearing, three trained members of the public, appointed to a local "children's panel", meet with the child, the parents and other professionals. The system operates on the basis of a division of powers between the hearing and the sheriff court. If there are disputed matters of fact or law, they must be determined by the court, meeting in private. The hearing's task is to decide whether a child needs compulsory measures of supervision and what measures are required. Procedure is informal, with encouragement for all to contribute to the discussion.

Although the whole focus of the proceedings is on the interests of the child, in 1975 a need was identified for an independent person to represent the interests of the child in cases where these were in conflict with the interests of the parent. This paralleled the introduction of the guardian ad litem in England and Wales. The new provisions were introduced in 1985,

The new Scottish person has come to be known as the safeguarder. The role has not been as developed nor as well used as the guardian ad litem in England and Wales. The criticisms set out above with regard to the representation of the interests of the child in private law apply equally here. There is no consistent matching of expertise with expectation. There is indeed no consistent expectation, so that safeguarders perform their roles according to their own professional backgrounds and predilections.

There has been an increasing interest in recent years in the role, such that the Scottish Office has set up a working group to look at the role and functions of the safeguarder. The 1995 Act widened the criteria for appointment. There is an expectation that they will be more frequently used in future.

The informality of the children's hearing system is designed to facilitate expression of views by children and parents. Indeed the Children's Hearing (Scotland) Rules oblige the hearing to 'give the child an opportunity to indicate whether he wishes to express his views.'[42] Children and parents are also entitled to take along any person as their representative to assist in discussion of the case.

Children and parents both have a right and obligation to attend the hearing, although excusal can be authorised in certain circumstances. An innovation of the 1995 Act is that the Hearing can now exclude a parent temporarily to allow the child to speak in private to it. The chairman must however tell the parents the substance of the discussion on their return.

This is a welcome change introduced in response to the expressed concerns of young people with experience of the care system. In the consultations leading to the passing of the 1995 Act, children in care were asked about their participation in children's hearings. Some spoke of the difficulty in expressing views in the presence of parents. One young person reported: 'I was stuck in the middle of mum and dad as if we were a cosy wee family. Nobody seemed to see the pressure my mum and dad were putting on me just by a movement or a look'.

There were also indications that, despite the relative informality of the hearings and their expressed aim of facilitating open discussion, young people experienced difficulty in speaking out. The consultation paper explains:

> The young people knew they have a right to take a friend along to the hearing, but most said that they were discouraged from doing this.
>
> 'Other people choose who is suitable. Care staff or your guidance. You're told you can't just bring a pal.'
>
> The youngsters wanted the choice about who represents them. Sometimes it might be someone from a voluntary organisation to give advice and support, sometimes they might want a legal person. Often their social worker would fit the bill, and sometimes they would need a friend to give them confidence to speak up.
>
> Most of the young people knew the word 'safeguarder' but were not clear about what it is or what it does. The safeguarder was just another part of the system.

There are separate provisions about representation of the views and interests of children in adoption proceedings and in proceedings for the transfer of parental responsibility to a local authority. These, too, involve curators ad litem and reporting officers. However, a similarity in name to those operating in private law proceedings does not imply a similarity of role. This adds to the present confusion.

The 1995 Act states some basic principles about the paramountcy of the child's interests, in private and public law, and about the need to take account of the child's views and give due weight to them. It creates a presumption that a child of 12 years or more is of sufficient age and maturity to form a view, although this does not mean that the views of children under that age are to be discounted.

As well as making reference to principles concerning the views and interests of children, the Act makes several references to people with a remit to represent them.

Section 91(4) allows rules to permit parties to the proceedings to be represented by someone who is neither an advocate nor a solicitor. Section 11(9) says that a child is not required to be legally represented in the proceedings if he or she does not wish to be.

Section 101 allows the Secretary of State to make regulations relating to establishment of a panel of persons from whom will be drawn curators ad litem and reporting officers under the adoption legislation and safeguarders appointed under the 1995 Act. The regulations may also make provision for appointment, qualification and training of such persons.

"Whilst these sections provide a basis for development of a more consistent system of child representation, they are far from comprehensive.

In short, Scotland is committed to the principles of regard to the interests and views of children, but still lacks a consistent and principled mechanism for putting these principles into practice.

3.5 Conclusion

There is in general no consistency of approach towards the participation of children and representation of their views and interests. France would appear to have the system most clearly rooted in principle. The English and Welsh system, particularly in the public law sphere, has much to commend it, although its approach is not carried through the rest of the legal system. The Canadian and Norwegian approaches are hesitant and patchy. The Scottish system has an emerging idea of where it wants to go, but does not yet know how to get there.

The states reported above may be well intentioned, but are mostly struggling to develop mechanisms which reflect and balance the rights of children to participate in terms of Article 12 and to have their interests promoted under Article 3.

The next chapter looks at an attempt by the Council of Europe to help its members address this issue.

Notes

1. UN paper CRC/C/8/Add. 7, Para. 63.
2. Ibid., Para. 65.
3. UN paper CRC/C/3/Add. 1, Para. 54.
4. UN paper CRC/C/8/Add. 8, Para. 31.

5. Children (Scotland) Act 1995, S. 6(1).
6. Social Work (Scotland) Act 1968, S. 20; Children Act 1989, S. 22.
7. UN paper CRC/C/8/Add. 7, Para. 68.
8. UN paper CRC/C/3/Add. 1, Para. 58.
9. Detrick (1991), pp. 132, 134.
10. Ibid., p. 272.
11. UN paper CRC/C/11/Add. 3, Para. 607.
12. Ibid., Para. 608.
13. Ibid., Para. 1176.
14. UN paper CRC/C/3/Add. 15, Para. 157.
15. UN paper CRC/C/SR 139, Para. 43.
16. UN paper CRC/C/3/Add. 15, Para. 87.
17. UN paper CRC/C/8/Add. 7, Para. 114.
18. Ibid., Para.115.
19. UN paper CRC/C/8/Add.7, Para. 69.
20. Ibid., Para. 213.
21. Ibid., Para. 214.
22. Ibid., Para. 216.
23. Ibid., Para. 116.
24. The substance of this was enacted for Northern Ireland in the Children (Northern Ireland) Order 1995.
25. UN paper CRC/C/11/Add. 1, Para. 3.23.
26. *The Children Act Advisory Committee Annual Report 1992–3*, Lord Chancellor's Department, p. 71.
27. Ibid., p. 32.
28. *The Children Act Advisory Committee Annual Report 1993–4*, Lord Chancellor's Department, p. 56.
29. Ibid., p. 54.
30. Children Act 1989, S.10(1)(2) and (5) [private law] and S.34(3)(b) [public law]; Procedure set out in Family Proceedings Rules 1991 rules 9.4 and 9.2A, and rules 4.10 and 4.12, and in the Family proceedings Courts (Children Act 1989) Rules 1991, rules 10 and 12. Information cited in *The Children Act Advisory Committee Annual Report 1993–4*, p. 46.
31. Re G (a minor) (care order) *The Times* 19 November 1992, FD; reported in *The Children Act Advisory Committee Annual Report 1992–3*, Lord Chancellor's Department, p. 71.
32. J v. Lancashire County Council 25 May 1993, unreported; in *The Children Act Advisory Committee Annual Report 1992–3*, p. 72.
33. *The Children Act Advisory Committee Annual Report 1993–4*, Lord Chancellor's Department, p. 45.
34. Re M (minors), 21 January 1993, unreported; in *The Children Act Advisory Committee Annual Report 1992–3*, p. 72.
35. *The Children Act Advisory Committee Annual Report 1992–3*, p. 73.
36. Law Reform (Parent and Child) (Scotland) Act 1986, S. 3(2).
37. Matrimonial Proceedings (Children) Act 1958, S. 11.
38. Children (Scotland) Act 1991, Schedule 4, Para. 53(3),

39. Act of Sederunt (Sheriff Court Ordinary Cause Rules) 1993.
40. Inserted into Rule 33.20 of the Act of Sederunt (Sheriff Court Ordinary Cause Rules) 1993 by Schedule 1, Paragraph 10 of the Act of Sederunt (Family Proceedings in the Sheriff Court) 1996.
41. Report of the Kilbrandon Commission, Cmnd 2306, (1964), *Children and Young Persons: Scotland*.
42. The Children's Hearing (Scotland) Rules 1996, Rule 15.
43. (1994) *Scotland's Children - Speaking Out: Young People's Views on Child Care Law in Scotland*, HMSO, Edinburgh.

Chapter 4

◆

THE EUROPEAN CONVENTION ON THE EXERCISE OF CHILDREN'S RIGHTS

4.1   Introduction

The Council of Europe welcomed the passing of the UN Convention on the Rights of the Child, and resolved to help its members fulfil their obligations to implement it.[1] This was consistent with the Council's aim to achieve greater unity between its members.[2]

Accordingly, the Parliamentary Assembly of the Council set in motion the drafting of a procedural convention with the aim of supplementing the UN Convention. This new Convention has been passed by the Council of Europe and opened for signature and ratification on 25 January 1996. It comes into force three months after receipt of the third ratification, inclusive of at least two member states of the Council of Europe. No reservations are permissible, so states must accept or reject the Convention as a whole.

Whilst it applies primarily to proceedings before a judicial authority, Article 11 obliges parties to the Convention to consider extending some of its provisions to matters affecting children which are not the subject of proceedings.

Chapter III of the Convention provides for the establishment of a Standing Committee to monitor problems raised by it. The Committee may give opinions on matters of interpretation or implementation.

4.2   Proceedings Falling within the Scope of the European Convention

The European Convention is effective only in relation to 'family proceedings' before a 'judicial authority'. Both of these terms are defined in the Convention. A 'judicial authority' is defined by Article 2 as ' a court or an administrative authority having equivalent powers'. The term 'family proceedings' is expanded upon in Article 1.3, which states that: 'For the purposes of this convention proceedings before a judicial authority affecting children are family proceedings, in particular those involving the exercise of parental responsibilities such as residence and access to children.'

The Explanatory Report attached to the Convention sets out examples of categories of cases which might fall into this category. These include cases regarding:

- custody;
- residence;
- access;
- questions of parentage;
- legitimacy (declaration, contestation);
- adoption;
- legal guardianship;
- administration of property of children;
- care procedures;
- removal or restriction of parental responsibilities;
- protection from cruel and degrading treatment; and
- medical treatment.

On signature or ratification, states must submit a declaration identifying at least three categories of cases to which the Convention will apply. They are free to specify more or to add others later.

Despite its emphasis on formal proceedings, the European Convention is at pains to point out that this does not imply that formal procedures are the best way to resolve family problems. The Preamble also states that: 'In the event of conflict it is desirable for families to try to reach agreement before bringing the matter before a judicial authority.' Article 13 obliges parties to encourage the provision of mediation and other processes aimed at keeping disputes about children out of court.

It should be recalled that the UN Committee, in its review of the Initial Report by Norway on its implementation of the UN Convention (see 2.4.4 above), appeared concerned that the child's views might be excluded if such diversionary measures were limited to involvement of parents. Whilst the European Convention does not oblige states to extend its provisions to such non-judicial processes, Article 11 does oblige them to consider doing so.

It is arguable that, in its failure to make extension to non-judicial processes obligatory, the European Convention undermines the more comprehensive approach of the UN Convention.

4.3   Children Falling within its Scope

The European Convention applies to children up to the age of 18 years. The explanatory report addresses the issues of:

1. children attaining full or partial legal capacity before that age. Where they are involved in proceedings contemplated in the Convention, it is anticipated that they will still benefit from the kind of help with court procedures which it envisages; and
2. children in states where the age of majority is above 18 years. Whilst the Convention does not strictly apply to them, it is hoped that they will continue to enjoy the benefits of it.

Whilst the Convention applies to all children under 18, a more mature group is singled out for additional rights. This group is distinguished by having 'sufficient understanding.' The criteria for determining this is left to the internal law of the parties to the Convention.

4.4   The Main Provisions of the European Convention

Article 2 sets out the Convention's primary objective:

> The object of the present convention is, in the best interests of children, to promote their rights, to grant them procedural rights and to facilitate the exercise of these rights by ensuring that children are, themselves or through other persons or bodies, informed and allowed to participate in proceedings affecting them before a judicial authority.

The following is a summary of the Convention's main provisions insofar as they relate to the participation of children. A distinction is made between those matters to which states are committed as a result of ratification, and those which they are committed only to consider. The relevant Article of the Convention is placed in brackets. Where a provision is marked ★, this means that it applies only to those children regarded as having sufficient understanding.

4.5 Children's Views

Parties are committed to:

- consulting the child and allowing him or her to express their views (3)★ and (6b)★;
- giving due weight to the views expressed by the child (6c);
- informing the child of the possible consequences of compliance with those views or of any decision (3)★; and
- consulting the child in person in appropriate cases, unless this would be 'manifestly contrary to the best interests of the child'. If necessary, the consultation may be carried out in private. It may be conducted by the judicial authority itself, or through other persons or bodies. The manner of consultation must be appropriate to the child's understanding. (6b)★. Paragraph 46 of the Explanatory Report points out that privacy does not necessarily imply confidentiality. Internal law may provide for parties to have access to relevant parts of this information.

Parties are committed to considering:

- giving children a right to apply to be assisted by an appropriate person of their choice in order to help them express their views (5a).

Paragraph 55 of the Explanatory Report notes that children are also free to refuse to express their views.

4.6 Provision of Information

Parties are committed to:

- giving all relevant information to the child (3)★ and ensuring the child has received it (6b)★. Paragraph 44 of the Explanatory Report notes that 'This may be particularly important when the child does not have a representative who is subject to the duties of Article 10, and the judicial authority has reason to believe that the holders of parental responsibilities have not given this information to the child. If the child has not been provided with this information the judicial authority should, where appropriate, inform the child or arrange for the child to be informed.'

'Relevant information' is defined by Article 2d to mean: 'information which is appropriate to the age and understanding of the child, and which will be given to enable the child to exercise his or her rights fully unless the provision of such information were manifestly contrary to the welfare of the child.'

- making sure that judicial authorities have enough information to enable them to make a decision in the best interests of the child, and obliging them to obtain further information if necessary (6a).

4.7   Representatives for Children

Parties are committed to:

- provision of 'special representatives' for children where there is a conflict of interest between the children and those having parental responsibilities. The child may request a representative (4.1)*, or the judicial authority may provide one on its own initiative (9.1).

Parties are committed to considering:

- giving power to the judicial authority to appoint a 'separate representative' (in appropriate cases a lawyer) to represent a child, even where there is no conflict of interest (9.2);
- giving children the right to apply themselves or through other persons or bodies for the appointment of a 'separate representative', in appropriate cases a lawyer (5b); and
- giving children the right to appoint their 'own representative' (5c). Paragraph 42 of the Explanatory Report notes that 'Even where a child has the right to choose a representative the judicial authority is not bound to accept an unsuitable person as the representative of the child.'

The Convention speaks of a 'special representative' , 'separate representative' and 'own representative'. The only word which is defined is 'representative' , therefore the qualifiers must relate to the circumstances of appointment rather than the substance of the role.

'Representative' is defined by Article 2c to mean: 'a person, such as a lawyer, or a body appointed to act before a judicial authority on behalf of a child'.

It would appear that the 'special representative' is appointed in cases of a conflict of interest between the child and the holder of parental responsibilities. The 'separate representative' is appointed by the judicial authority where there is no conflict of interest. The 'own representative' is appointed by the child.

The role of the representative is set out in Article 10, as follows:

> In the case of proceedings before a judicial authority affecting a child the representative shall, unless this would be manifestly contrary to the best interests of the child:
> a) provide all relevant information to the child, if the child is considered by internal law as having sufficient understanding;
> b) provide explanations to the child if the child is considered by internal law as having sufficient understanding, concerning the possible consequences of compliance with his or her views and the possible consequences of any action by the representative; and
> c) determine the views of the child and present these views to the judicial authority.

Article 10.2 obliges states to consider extending these responsibilities to the holders of parental responsibilities.

4.8   Party Status

Parties are committed to consider:

- giving children the right to exercise some or all of the rights of parties to such proceedings (5d).

4.9   Critique

The European Convention puts a high priority on the presentation of children's views. There is, nevertheless, a possibility of children not being consulted. This could be because:

- they are regarded as lacking sufficient understanding, and therefore no active steps are taken to ascertain their views, although there is a passive obligation to consider views expressed; or

- they have sufficient understanding, but a representative has judged that determining and/or presenting the views of the child would be manifestly contrary to the child's best interests.

The second scenario could open the door to abrogation of a child's right to express his or her views. There should at least be a mechanism for challenging the judgements inherent in these exceptions, or they may be open to misuse or abuse.

Even this possibility implies that a child must at least be informed that there is an issue in relation to which he or she has a right to be consulted. Does this interests-based qualification envisage a situation in which the child's interests are held to justify a complete exclusion of the child, even from knowledge of what is taking place? Such an approach would not appear to be justified by the terms of the UN Convention (see 2.3.4 above). The views of professionals and young people on this issue are set out in Chapter 5 of this book.

The Convention proceeds on the presumption that participation does not imply the actual presence of the child at the proceedings. There is a tendency to assume that it does. Natural justice may argue in favour of the presence of children, especially where they express a desire to attend. It may also be essential to full participation where the forum concerned is one in which it is expected that positions and proposals might change in response to the discussion of parties present.

The Convention proceeds on the basis that children with sufficient understanding should possess the 'relevant information' on which the decision will be based. Both the definition of 'relevant information' and the role of the representative in providing it are subject to qualifications rooted in concern for the welfare of the child. This might be reasonable, providing there was an opportunity for a child to challenge this decision. As will be seen in 5.4.6 below, a child may feel more traumatised by being told that there is information about him or her that is so awful that access is denied, than by having access to the information concerned.

The role of the representative as set out in the Convention would appear to be clearly focused on presentation of the child's views rather than safeguarding the child's interests. The qualification concerning actions that would be 'manifestly contrary to the best interest of the child' does not appear to envisage a change in role as such to that of a person representing the interests of the child. It seems rather to act as an exceptional qualifier to each of the components of the role. This blurs the clarity of the role and opens the door to abrogation of the rights of children.

Confusion is compounded by further discussion of the role in Paragraphs 54 to 56 of the Explanatory Report, which contradicts the Convention's assumption of a focus on the child's views. Paragraph 55 says that: 'Determining the views of the child does not necessarily only mean speaking to the child and asking the child to express views verbally but also includes 'observations' of the child by a representative or by, for example, an expert medical practitioner.' This makes the representative a possible interpreter of the views of the child. Moreover, the paragraph adds that: 'representatives may give their own views on the best interests of children'. This extends the potential remit of the representative. It appears as somewhat of an afterthought, and yet it is of crucial importance to the integrity and consistency of the representative and the rights of children.

This 'afterthought' is the only reference to the representation of children's interests in judicial proceedings. It may be that this is not seen to be a problem in systems or procedures based on an inquisitorial philosophy. It could well be a problem in adversarial systems. Even if the basis of the decision will be the best interests of the child, the court will be limited to consideration of information presented to it by warring adult parties, or contained in reports written by persons such as court welfare officers who do not have the rights of parties to the proceedings.

The Explanatory Report assumes that representation of a child's views is quite consistent with expression by the representative of his or her own views, which might contradict those of the child. Yet, insertion of this latter possibility radically alters the nature of the role. It is submitted that there is a radical difference between *representing* a person's views and *presenting* them in the context of a report or statement which advocates something contrary.

The failure to recognise this means that the interaction between the representation of interests and views is not addressed. This is important because some procedures do operate on a model which embraces both functions and there are questions about the propriety of this approach.

The lack of a focus on the representation of interests is also of concern because the most potent provisions of the Convention apply only to those determined by internal law as having 'sufficient understanding.' This gives a lot of scope to states. Whilst it is hoped that good faith will avoid establishment of unduly restrictive criteria, the Convention does leave itself vulnerable to this possibility. The interests of children deemed not to have 'sufficient understanding' are not adequately addressed. It is also hoped that there would have been some expectation of the appointment of a representative to conduct the case on the child's behalf on the basis of the representation of the child's interests, at least in cases where the interests of the child were in conflict with those of the holders of parental responsibility. However, although the criterion for the appointment of a 'special representative' is the existence of a conflict of interest, the stated focus of the role is on representation of views.

Article 1.6 of the Convention states that: 'Nothing in this convention shall prevent Parties from applying rules more favourable to the promotion and exercise of children's rights.' The Convention therefore represents the minimum standard which it is expected states will achieve. States are free to adopt additional measures which are more conducive to the promotion of children's rights.

States which have ratified the UN Convention must be wary of assuming that compliance with the European Convention fulfils their UN obligations. The European Convention falls short of the standards set by the UN Convention. Failure to acknowledge this could lead to the UN Convention being undermined.

Notes

1. Introduction to the *Explanatory Report to the European Convention on the Exercise of Children's Rights*, Para. 4.
2. Member States of the Council of Europe on 1 September 1995: Albania, Andorra, Austria, Belgium, Bulgaria, Cyprus, Czech Republic, Denmark, Estonia, Finland,

France, Germany, Greece, Hungary, Iceland, Ireland, Italy, Latvia, Liechtenstein, Lithuania, Luxembourg, Malta, Moldova, Netherlands, Norway, Poland, Portugal, Romania, San Marino, Slovakia, Slovenia, Spain, Sweden, Switzerland, Turkey, United Kingdom.

Chapter 5

◆

ATTITUDES TO CHILDREN'S PARTICIPATION

5.1   Introduction

How is the relationship between the views and interests of children perceived by adults working with children and by children themselves?

Awareness of attitudes is an essential preliminary to effective implementation of the UN Convention. If the Convention is misunderstood or disliked, its principles will be subverted in practice. If the Convention is accepted in principle but implemented insensitively, it will lose credibility and children will be disadvantaged.

As discussed in 2.4.3 above, France's Initial Report to the UN included a helpful reflection upon the place of children's views in the decision-making process. The French Government also made reference to the importance of 'attitudes of mind' with regard to the participation of children.

It seemed clear, from the author's experience, that many adults had concerns about involving children in decision-making. There was a perception that, if applied to all situations, it might result in children being given inappropriate information, inappropriate responsibility, and inappropriate involvement in intimidating and adversarial processes.

From the children's point of view, it is often stated that children are ambivalent about participation. With regard to formal processes, it is said that they do not always like attending them, but neither do they like the idea of people gathering together to talk about them behind their backs. With regard to informal processes, it is often stated that children may in fact want their voice to be heard, but that they sacrifice this option for the sake of harmony and to avoid causing emotional pain to adults.

In order to test this, a survey questionnaire was sent to 20 senior professionals in Scotland involved with children in the fields of social work, law and psychology, including some organisations dealing with child welfare. They were invited to express their views about children and young people being involved in decisions, and whether they should have a right to be present at meetings and to get access to all the information the adults had. They were also asked about mechanisms for determining whether a child was capable of forming an opinion, and how the weight to be given to that opinion should be determined. A copy of the survey questionnaire is set out as an Appendix to this book.

There were 15 responses. Of these, 11 took the form of personal interviews based on the questionnaire, and four were written responses. Those consulted had the following professional status:

children's panel member[1]	1
children's panel reporter[2]	1
child psychologist	2
safeguarder	2
sheriff	2
social worker	3
solicitor	2
voluntary children's organisation	6

(Note: the numbers add up to more than 15 as some respondents had more than one role.)

In addition, four young people from the Who Cares? Scotland organisation were interviewed. This voluntary organisation works to promote the rights of young people in care. All of the young people had experience of being in care.

The survey was designed as a qualitative rather than a quantitative exercise. Numbers were small and therefore a numerical count of responses would have no statistical significance. Accordingly, no reference is made to the numbers giving the same or similar answers. Where there appeared to be a consistent strength of feeling, this is indicated in general terms.

5.2 Adults' Attitudes to Participation in General

When asked whether they were in basic agreement with the participation principle set out in Article 12, all adults indicated that they were. Some agreed because they saw it as a basic right; others because they said it led to better, more enforceable decisions. This latter view was expressed by both of the Sheriffs interviewed, one of whom commented:

> A child is not an object but a participant. It is entirely proper that a child should feel part of the process even if their view is not a deciding factor in the end. If a child is of a certain age – 13, 14 15 – an order won't work if the child disagrees with it. The views of a child of that age may be determinative.

It was also the view of an interviewee with extensive experience of the children's hearing system:

> You can't come to a firm decision without listening to the child's views. Even if you can't give them what they want, you have to listen to what they want and why it is important to them. It is sometimes difficult to do this. Children can usually justify why they want things.

Social workers expressed the view that children needed to know what was going on and to have decisions explained to them. Failure to take account of children's views showed a lack of respect for children and could alienate them.

From a pragmatic point of view, social workers themselves felt that the existence of a right to participate would: 'redress the tendency of social workers to make decisions based on their own assessments without really having a good look at what the child is saying'. There was said to be: 'a danger of adults making assumptions without checking the matter out with the child'.

Of the two psychologists interviewed, one expressed some reservations about participation: 'because a child may have difficulties in expressing his view in a way that the nature of that view is understood'. The other pointed out that: 'Ascertainment of children's views makes it easier to prepare children for a decision that goes against their wishes and to explain to them why it was considered to be in their interests to take this decision'.

A solicitor commented that: 'One can't take exception to the principle; it's the translating it into reality that is difficult. The reality lies in the fact that the child will remain part of that family. If that reality is not taken into account, it can make things worse for the child rather than better, and raise expectations that cannot be fulfilled'. The solicitor's concerns centred on the reality of current legal mechanisms set within the context of an adversarial system which posed problems for participation by children. Within that context, the physical presence of the child might be positively damaging.

This last concern was echoed in the responses of all adults surveyed. They felt that there were circumstances in which children and young people should not be present when a decision was being made, but should participate in other ways, for example, by writing their own reports, or by having someone else express their views to the meeting. Nevertheless, many emphasised that excluding young people should be the exception rather than the rule.

Most also thought there were cases in which adults should keep information back from children and young people, even if it was relevant to a decision being made about them in which they had a right to be involved. This did not mean that the information should be kept back for ever. It was more often a question of deciding how and when to give it.

The following sections will look in greater detail at the responses to the questions about the physical presence of a child at the decision-making forum, and access to information, as well as the other questions posed in the survey.

5.3   The Presence of the Child

All of those surveyed felt that there were circumstances in which adults needed to be able to discuss issues relating to the child without the child being present. When asked to give examples, their responses could be grouped into scenarios where it was felt that:

1.   the meeting required to discuss information, knowledge of which might damage the child;

2. the meeting required to discuss information which was private to others;
3. the actions of others at the meeting might distress the child; and
4. the very nature of the process was such that being present was likely to confuse, distress or damage the child.

5.3.1 Knowledge of the Issues to be Discussed would be Damaging.

Several respondents referred specifically to issues surrounding serious illness in the family, particularly HIV/AIDS, as a justification for excluding a child from a discussion. It was recognised that the child would need to know at some time. One had to ensure that the child was told at the right time, in the right place; was adequately prepared beforehand and supported afterwards. An experienced children's panel member related the following case as an example:

> A seven-year-old's mother was terminally ill with cancer. The parents wanted to tell the Children's Hearing because they wanted a particular network of care for the child, which was different from what was being recommended by the social worker. A psychologist had assessed that the child was not yet ready to know about her mother's illness. She would clearly have to know eventually, but needed time. The children's hearing was not the time nor the place to find out. Had the child been older and insisting on attending, the Hearing would have continued the case until the child was told.

This scenario highlights the need for those organising children's hearings and other fora working within time limits to ensure that meetings are held within a timescale that allows for a continuation to meet this kind of eventuality.

Exposure to discussions about child abuse was also thought to be a possible reason for excluding the child. An example was given by an experienced social worker of a case in which a child was excluded from a discussion against his expressed wishes:

> The child was excluded because it was felt that the quality of the discussion on the abuse (where, how and by whom) might further distress him, and because there was a possibility that the parent might be charged. Children in these circumstances often carry an enormous burden of guilt. Participation might have made the child feel more guilty. In this case, the issues were

discussed with the child and the reasons for excluding him. The child was not happy about this and indicated that he would rather be present. The workers were not sure whether this was a real expression of his views or a piece of bravado.

This worker felt that, on balance, it was sometimes justifiable to exclude a child against the child's expressed wishes, because the level of guilt being suffered by the young person was already enormous.

A case in which a young person's wishes were adhered to against the advice of professionals involved with her was referred to by a respondent with experience of the children's hearing system:

A very disturbed 15-year-old had been the victim of abuse. She said she wanted to be present at the Children's Hearing. Everyone involved, including her safeguarder, said it was not a good idea. Nevertheless, she did attend, ran out in the middle of the Hearing and smashed up the office.

Despite that experience, the respondent felt that, on balance, there was more to gain by emphasising the right to attend than not.

Abuse was also seen as a possible justification for excluding a child from a meeting where the abuse was not of the child excluded, but another child. A sheriff referred to the possibility of a child being involved in proceedings on the ground that the parent had sexually abused another child. This might be a ground for referral of the abuser's children to children's hearing. Whilst the child referred would clearly have to be given some information about why this was happening, it was questionable whether he or she should be present to hear all the details of the abuse.

5.3.2 *Information Discussed is Private to Others*

Where the discussion might touch on private or intimate information, for example, about the parents' sexuality, it was felt that there should be a possibility of excluding a child from part of a meeting.

5.3.3 *Actions of Others at the Meeting might Distress the Child*

This is the unpredictable element of meetings. Although one can take steps to decide beforehand what information a child should be given or who should be present, people can behave in unexpected ways. A parent might be drunk and belligerent and embarrass and frighten the child. Professionals might express negative comments about the child or the parent, which it is difficult for the child to hear. The following were presented as examples:

> A child was present at a Children's Hearing where a father unexpectedly said 'By the way – I'm not fighting for all the children. You can keep her. I don't want her back.' The girl in question was devastated. The panel members were upset, but acknowledged that the child was possibly aware of the tension anyway. [children's panel member]

> In the course of a meeting, a headteacher announced that the mother was alcoholic. The child didn't know. The mother got up and ran out of the room crying, and then the child got up and ran out crying. The child then had to deal with the mother's upset. Often, children are given unrealistic responsibility for their parents; this adds to it. [psychologist]

> A nine-year-old whose mother had custody said he wanted to stay with his father and expressed fear of his mother. The solicitor was aware of the need to avoid alienating the mother in the interest of the boy and his future relationship with her, and therefore tried to impart the information to the sheriff in a non-alienating way. The sheriff interviewed the child and told the court all the details of what the child had said – some of it very distressing for the mother. The sheriff was quite punitive in approach to the mother who initially responded by expressing a desire to cut off all contact with the child. The solicitor was glad that the child was not there to witness the mother's distress and her initial emotive over-reaction which the child might have had difficulty seeing in context. On the other hand, the solicitor felt there was perhaps a need to acknowledge that that the child might well be accustomed to this kind of scene and worse. [solicitor]

The dynamic of a meeting is also unpredictable. A psychologist noted that meetings might be full of indecision, giving the child a feeling of insecurity; a feeling that adults don't know what to do. At the end of the day, the conclusion might be that there is no solution, but that a particular decision is 'the best fit'.

The relevance of this aspect might vary with the maturity of the child. A voluntary organisation pointed out that it should be reassuring for young people to know what options have been considered and why the decisions have been made. Indeed, if this need is not recognised, young people will feel alienated from the process and will rebel against it.

Older children may well have lost any illusions of adult omnipotence and be more appreciative of an honest assessment of limited options than a pretence that something that was clearly not a good fit was the best resolution.

5.3.4   *Presence at the Process would be Confusing, Distressing or Damaging*

A voluntary organisation pointed to parental separation as involving issues which might sometimes have to be discussed without the child being present. When adults are discussing consequences and practical arrangements, there were said to be occasions when it would be inappropriate and even damaging for the child to be present. This applied particularly where there was huge conflict. Even where this was not the case, the difficulties of the child could be made worse because of the conflict of loyalties the child was bound to feel.

This need was acknowledged by a sheriff who indicated that there was a need to consider the extent to which the child was involved in mediation. Parents needed some space to discuss things without the child being present. There was also a need to take the pressure off the child, who might feel he or she was at fault for causing the conflict.

It was generally felt that there were parts of the discussion which children did not need to hear, so long as they had access to some information relevant to the outcome for them.

A question was asked about what would happen if adults felt the discussion needed to enter areas which the child should not hear and it was not possible to discuss the matter without the child being present. A psychologist replied that, if the felt need to exclude the child was not met, more sensitive people might hold back from saying things that ought to be said because they would be afraid of upsetting the child. On the other hand, less sensitive people might say things that would upset the child.

5.3.5 *Young People's Views on Presence*

Reasons for excluding children and young people from meetings discussing matters affecting them were put to a group of four young people from Who Cares? Scotland, an organisation promoting the rights of children and young people in care.

The group were strongly of the opinion that young people who wished to attend meetings should be allowed to do so. They were willing to concede that there might be some instances in which younger children might be excluded, but emphasised that this should be the exception rather than the rule. If such a situation arose, the wishes of the child about attending should be taken very seriously and the child's maturity and ability to understand and cope with the situation assessed.

Whilst preferring to rely on the needs of the individual child, they acknowledged that there was some merit in setting a benchmark age, and felt that 12 years was appropriate. Again they stressed that this was of value only insofar as it prevented adults from excluding young people aged 12 and over, who should have an absolute right to attend. It should not be used to dilute the rights of under-12s.

The following were their responses to some specific scenarios:

- A fear on the professionals' part that parents might be drunk or aggressive and embarrass or distress the child.

  The young people felt that the decision about whether to attend should be the child's. They would probably have seen and experienced this behaviour already. At least at the meeting they would feel safe. If the meeting is to discuss the child's future, if anyone had to be excluded, it should be the parents.

- When information private to the parents is being discussed, for example concerning their sexuality.

  It depends how serious it is. If it is about someone being gay or a prostitute, for example, the child might have to know at some point anyway. It might be good for the parents to be honest with the children. Sometimes adults don't give children the credit they deserve about understanding things. On the other hand they did recognise that there might be a few cases in which it was not appropriate for a young child to attend. They looked at it from the perspective of the parents and agreed that, if they were the parents, there were some things they would not want young children to hear about them. There was no real defining age. It depended on the child.

- When adults intend splitting up and are discussing what arrangements might be made for a child, for example who to live with, access visits, and so on.

  The young people's initial reaction was that the child should be involved in the whole process. Most children can sense beforehand if their parents are going to split up. They did recognise that this might involve some 'tricky' situations in which the child was 'in the middle'. Children should make up their own minds about whether to be present.

- When people in a meeting express negative attitudes about a child or his or her parents. It might not be good for a child to hear this.

  The young people said they were going to get negative attitudes expressed about them anyway. If there weren't any, they wouldn't need the meeting at all.

- The case of a sheriff in court giving a mother a severe telling-off. She was so upset she said she never wanted to see the child again. She didn't really mean what she had said, but if the child had been present, would the child have been able to understand that?

  The young people said that parents say that kind of thing anyway. One young person related his experience of being told the same while quite a young child by a parent, who eventually re-established some contact. He said he did understand.

- When meetings are full of indecision. It can give a child a feeling of insecurity if he or she thinks adults don't know what to do.

  The young people swept aside the concerns about feelings of insecurity. 'You are more likely to be angry if the adults were all fighting about your life and no-one was asking what you wanted.' This could make you 'confused, angry, stressed-out and rebellious'. In any event, being involved in decisions and being realistic about options helped to prepare you for when you were 16 or 17 and had to make decisions for yourself.

- Meetings about long-term policy can be confusing for a young child who can't understand the idea of something happening in six months' time.

  The young people thought it was a question of putting the information to the child in an appropriate way and reminding them of it from time to time in a way that made sense to them, rather than just saying 'in six months' time'. Adults need to work on the information and build on it.

- The case of a very disturbed young person who insisted on attending a Children's Hearing although the adults involved tried to dissuade her because they thought she would be unable to cope. She attended the hearing, ran out half way through and trashed the office. Should she have been allowed to attend?

The young people thought it should still be up to the young person to decide whether to attend. They added that 'Maybe what made her crack up was that people didn't believe in her.' Adults should tell the young person what to expect and not to get too agitated. It was a risk you took at all panels. If it was about you, you had a right to be there.

- Where abuse of the child is being discussed. The discussion might distress the child. If there is a suggestion that the parent might be charged, the child might already be experiencing feelings of guilt, and taking part might make those feelings worse.

  The young people stressed that it all came down to communication. If children think they are going to be stressed, they should be allowed to sit it out. A lot of work had to be done putting the guilt where it belongs – each and every day – so that it becomes less of an issue.

- If a child has been referred to a children's hearing because his or her parent is accused of abusing another child. Adults might not want the child to be present while the abuse is being discussed.

  There was debate about this issue, as the young people pointed out that the counterbalancing issue for them was the confidentiality of the abused child and whether this was breached by allowing children of the abuser to be party to a discussion about the details of the abuse. At the same time, they felt that it was possible that the abuser's children had also been abused and hearing the discussion might give them the courage to speak up and also enable them to assess the risk to themselves and better protect themselves from it. There would be a need to explain something, even to a younger child.

- When there is anything that would unnecessarily upset or harm a child.

  The young people's response was that it wasn't possible to 'wrap people up in cotton wool'.

- Some adults were unable to think of any cases, but felt there should be a possibility of excluding young people in case circumstances came up where it was felt best to do so.

  There was a division of opinion. One young person felt it should always be up to the child. If children felt they could handle it, they should be allowed to go. Another felt there might be some cases where if she were the parent of a young child, she would not want the child to be present to listen to the discussion. There should certainly be an absolute right to attend at the age of 12 years old. One thought the age should be 10. However, exclusion from meetings should be an exception. It should still be your basic right to attend, even if you were only five or six years old.

5.3.6 *Conclusion*

The importance of attendance in ensuring full participation varies according to the kind of forum involved. Less formal fora such as social work reviews and Children's Hearings aim to engage those present in a dialogue. The underlying expectation is that what people say can affect the outcome of that meeting.

Court procedures are rather different. Unless cited as a witness, the child will not be expected to contribute personally. On the other hand, the child might wish to be present to hear what is said as this might affect the child's contribution through his or her representatives. The right to attend is therefore of more immediate significance in informal fora than in court proceedings, but may still be important in the latter.

The conclusion from the above would appear to be that children do not necessarily have to be present in order to participate; indeed, sometimes their presence could be inhibiting to adults and damaging to the children. On the other hand, adults should be very slow to exclude a young person who expresses a wish to attend. The presumption should lie in favour of acceding to the young person's wishes, with the onus lying on adults to justify their exclusion. In some fora there may be merit in giving children an absolute right to attend from a certain age.

Whilst this would seem to indicate that the presence of the child is not a *necessary* condition for participation (at least in terms of the UN Convention) neither should adults assume that it is a *sufficient* condition for participation. Some respondents emphasised the point that the fact that a child is present does not necessarily mean that he or she has fully understood and participated in the decision. There is a danger of tokenism.

A social worker pointed out that presence does not mean there is meaningful participation. He cited the case of an adolescent who was present throughout a meeting to decide whether he should go into a hostel. Later in life, the young man reported that he felt he did not have any real say in the matter; that he felt coerced by adults. The truth is that there probably was not anywhere else for him to go, so options were limited. Even so, the matter was clearly discussed in a way that made the young person feel excluded. The social worker felt that it might be advisable for children in these situations to have advocates. He commented that we must be careful not to assume that bringing a child or young person into a meeting is going to make everything all right. This sentiment was also expressed by a psychologist who commented: 'Sometimes at the end of a meeting, the chair asks the child – 'Is that all right with you?' It is then noted that the child agrees with the plan of action'.

5.4   Withholding Information from a Child

Respondents were asked whether it was ever legitimate to withhold relevant information from a child in order to protect the child's interests. 'Relevant information' was described as information relevant to a decision concerning a child.

All respondents felt there was a case for withholding information in some circumstances. However, it was a case of waiting for the appropriate time and place to give the information that was at issue. Respondents were reluctant to suggest that any information should be permanently withheld. It was acknowledged that, by the time the appropriate moment to impart it was reached, the decision under consideration might have been made. This would mean that the child's participation would be limited to the extent that he or she did not possess all the relevant facts. As an employee of a child welfare organisation noted:

> If you had quite a young child whose parents were dying of AIDS, obviously the child would have to have the information at some point, but major decisions might have to be made before it is appropriate to tell the child. I can't think of any information that should be permanently withheld. Even if a child was the result of an incestuous rape, they might have to know sometime.

A psychologist commented:

> The general principle should be that the information should be withheld if it is something that the child is not ready to hear, and knowing it would

cause unnecessary additional trauma and unhappiness. The child has as much a right to be protected from information as to be exposed to it. Children have no power, so why burden them with responsibility?

On the other hand, one should not assume that, by not sharing information with a child, one is protecting him from the painful reality that lies behind it. A respondent from a voluntary organisation commented:

> Children may be adept at picking up non-verbal clues. If they pick something up in this way and adults don't help them place it in a verbal framework, it can make things worse for the child. It is important to check out at an early stage what the child already knows.

Justifications for withholding information could be grouped under the following headings:

1. Possession of the information would be damaging to the child.
2. Possession of the information would put undue pressure on the child.
3. The information was private to others.

Headings 1 and 3 mirror two of the justifications given for excluding a child from a meeting.

5.4.1 Possession of the Information would be Damaging to a Child

In matters of separation and divorce, there was a feeling that knowledge of the details of the relationship breakdown could be damaging to a child. A worker for a voluntary organisation commented:

> In separation and divorce, it is important that the child has some information but it should be sifted by adults rather than given direct. It may be appropriate to withhold some information on, for example, the reasons for the separation – if the father has a string of affairs and gone off to live with a woman down the road. What information is given and the way it is provided should be governed by the age of the child. The question is not just what to tell them, but how to tell them.

The existence of terminal illness, in a parent or a child, was also held as justifying withholding information in some circumstances.

A respondent working with the children's hearing system related a case concerning a child living with foster parents. The plan was for him to come home. The week before the Hearing at which it was proposed to send him home, the mother changed her mind. She told panel members that she had just discovered she had terminal cancer.

Another case referred to concerned the illness of a child. This was known as the case of Child B in England in 1995. The 11-year-old was suffering from leukaemia. The health authority had decided to discontinue treatment, and the father was challenging this decision. There was considerable press interest in the case. The respondent suggested one could argue that because of the media hype it would have been unfair to have told her, at that moment, that she was the subject of the debate.

Issues concerned with parentage were also raised. Another children's hearing case concerned a child referred for poor school attendance. It emerged in a social work report that the child's 'father' was not in fact his biological parent. There was no intent to withhold the information permanently, but to be sensitive as to when and how the child was to be told.

The damage to the child might be compounded if the information revealed that the child had been conceived as a result of rape, and the rapist father was in prison or in a mental hospital. A sheriff responding felt that, whilst this might be relevant background information, it was not something one would want to reveal to a child not yet old enough to understand.

A social worker referred to the 'human' aspect involved in deciding whether to withhold information from children: 'It is definitely done, although I am not always sure that it's to protect the interests of the child. Workers feel the need to protect the child. It's the 'feeling' bit. In child protection, there are not many cases where the child should not hear and be helped to understand'.

Even if information is considered as possibly damaging, there may be ways of presenting it which minimise that damage. Whether this is a compromise worth making, out of respect for the child's right to the fullest participation possible, is a decision that would have to be made on a case-by-case basis. A psychologist suggested:

If the child requests information that expert adults deem might be damaging, we must find ways of making it undamaging by the way we present it, like giving a pill with a coating on it so that it doesn't burn the throat on the way down. For example, if the mother is a prostitute, give the child not only that information, but information that allows her to accept it without damage to her own self-esteem and to the relationship with her mother.

5.4.2   Possession of the Information would put Undue Pressure on a Child

There might be everyday situations in which information-giving was delayed in order to avoid putting pressure on a child. One example referred to by a voluntary organisation concerned a child who was about to sit an important exam. In this situation, one might feel justified in withholding distressing information until the exam was over.

Other situations were more exceptional and might have legal implications. In cases of alleged child abuse, there might be an embargo placed on a particular type of discussion between the alleged abuser and the child until a certain point was reached, for example a court hearing. The child might not be told what the parents had said about the allegation so that he or she was not bulldozed into seeing their view. Professionals would be trying to ensure that children did not succumb to attempts by alleged abusers to get them to retract their story. This was described as a classic situation.

Children whose parents are separating might also fall into this category. It has been suggested that once the influence of children's participation is appreciated by adults, warring adults might each put undue pressure on a child, whether by bribes, threats, misinformation or coaching, to encourage the child to support a particular adult view.

5.4.3   The information was Private to Others

Intimate details of the parents' relationship were felt to be something that might be kept from a child. There was some suggestion that the fact that the mother had been raped was also something private to her which the child should not necessarily be told.

A respondent familiar with the children's hearing system referred to circumstances in which references to an abusive relationship between the parents would be included in reports rather than discussed at the hearing. This was when there was a fear that a discussion would lead to the mother receiving further abuse on return to the home. One might want to keep this kind of information from the child.

A sheriff referred to a case of a 14-year-old finding out in the witness box that her mother had been pregnant by another man.

5.4.4 Who Should Decide whether Information should be Withheld from a Child?

Several respondents felt that the general responsibility for deciding what to tell a child should lie with the parents. When the matter came before a formal body, such as a court or children's hearing, then that body should make the decision according to specified criteria.

Sometimes parents forbid adults telling a child something which professionals feel the child had a need or a right to know. A social worker reported:

> Sometimes an embargo is placed by a mother, for example about who the father is. If the child is not asking it is difficult to do other than respect the mother's embargo. If the child asks, workers try to go back to the parents. There is a dilemma about telling against the wishes of caring parents; this can have consequences for the child, maybe because of the attitude of the parents. There was a case where the mother had Multiple Sclerosis and didn't want the child to know. After months of persuasion, she finally agreed to tell the child.

A worker from a voluntary organisation believed that parents should primarily be the ones deciding what information children should have. She acknowledged that children had rights under the UN Convention but pointed out:

> There is a difficulty in that parents have not really caught up with what the UN Convention expects them to do. We are in a transitional phase. Families

vary a lot in the way adults relate to each other and the extent to which children participate. In this transitional phase, there may be a case for someone outside this stressful family situation to be involved. I wouldn't go as far as saying that they should be able to overrule the parents. They would have to take account of the parent/child relationship and the impact on the child's perceptions of adults being in control; because basically you are saying that the adults are not in control.

These observations appear to express fears that if outsiders interfere too readily, this might undermine parental authority and damage the parent–child relationship.

When a formal body is involved, the rights of the child might be more clearly articulated. An analysis of responses concerning this question would suggest that:

1. The presumption should be in favour of giving information to the child. It should only be withheld as a result of a specific decision by an appropriate person. In a court situation that would be the sheriff.
2. Where parents objected to the child being given the information, the court should take that into account, but the decision should be based on the needs and rights of the child.
3. Where a decision to withhold information was made, the court should appoint a curator or safeguarder who would be able to represent the child's interests on the basis of receipt of all the relevant information, including that withheld from the child. In deciding whether to withhold information, the court might also seek the opinion of such a person.

5.4.5   How Information is Presented to a Child

Whilst not in concrete terms withheld, information might be effectively withheld if not presented in a way that the child can understand. Just as the presence of a child is neither a necessary nor sufficient condition for participation, neither is the service of a formal document in language that may be impenetrable even to most adults. Two comments on this emanated from people with experience of the Children's Hearing system:

- Reports are written for adults; we have to make them accessible to children.

81

- It is pretty horrendous that children get given the same grounds of referral to the children's hearing as the adults.

5.4.6   *Young People's Views on Withholding Information*

The following is a list of circumstances in which adults said they might feel justified in withholding information from a child or young person, together with the young people's response:

- Where it is alleged that a parent abused a child, the child might not be told what the parent said about the allegations in case the parent tries to bulldoze him or her into accepting their view.

  The young people recognised this was a difficult issue, but felt it was more relevant to being present at meetings with such parents than to access to information. They hoped the new Scottish provisions allowing children's hearings to exclude parents temporarily in order to hear the child would help to address this.
- If a parent does not want a child to know something, for example about who the father is. Should the child be given that information (1) if he or she doesn't ask; (2) if he or she does ask?

  The young people were divided on this, depending on their personal experience. One said it depended what the parents were like. He had kept back from asking his mother because he did not want to hurt her. She told him eventually herself. Another recalled the shock she had experienced at a Children's Hearing when an adult let slip the identity of her father. She had not known this before. She felt she should have been told in another way, and that young people did have the right to know.
- The child was conceived as a result of rape.

  The young people felt they would get to know some time, so it was best it was done in a proper way at a good time. They recognised that a younger child, for example a six-year-old, might not be able to make any sense of the information, and it might be more harmful for them to know.
- The parent has a terminal disease.

  The young people would want to know.
- The mother is a prostitute.

  The young people felt the children might need to know this, but it should be explained to them in a supportive way.

A general point expressed by the young people was that it can be very distressing and damaging to be told that there is some information about you which is so awful that you are not allowed access to it. Fear and uncertainty in this situation can be worse for the young person than knowing the information itself.

5.4.7   *Conclusion*

The following principles have been drawn from the above responses:

- The presumption should be in favour of passing on all relevant information to a child participating in a decision.
- Information should be sifted by a responsible person to determine what it is relevant for a child to know and whether knowledge of it might be damaging to a child.
- A responsible person should ascertain what a child already knows about the situation.
- In some situations, the 'responsible person' will be the child's parent or carer. There must be a method of challenging the parent's decision to withhold information if others feel that the child should have it. In formal situations, or where there is a conflict of interest, an independent person should be allocated this task.
- If it is felt some information might be damaging to a child, consideration should be given as to how it could be presented in a way that would make it easier for the child to accept without damage.
- There should be a possibility of withholding information – temporarily at least – in the interests of the child.
- If information is withheld from a child in the course of judicial or administrative proceedings, an independent person should be appointed to represent the interests of the child in those proceedings, in consultation with the child and with access to the information denied to the child.
- Before a meeting which a child will attend, a responsible person should scan available information, consider what a child already knows, identify any points of difficulty and recommend arrangements to address them.
- Wherever possible, meetings should be arranged within a timescale that allows the proceedings to be continued to allow a child to be informed and counselled on relevant information that might come to light during it. Difficulties could be encountered if an order required to be made or renewed within a tight timescale.
- Information should be presented to children in a way that is meaningful to them.

5.6 Is a Child Capable of Forming a View?

Respondents to the survey were asked whether there might be difficulties in ascertaining whether a child was capable of forming an opinion, and who ought to make that assessment. This is important because the ability to form a view is the trigger for activation of the rights set out in Article 12 of the UN Convention.

5.5.1 *Views and Opinions*

An initial question arose about whether views and opinions were the same thing. The published versions of the UN Convention would seem to indicate that they are. Article 12 speaks in terms of the child's 'views', whilst the accompanying 'unofficial summary' refers to the child's 'opinion'. It is respect for the child's opinion which is often spoken of as the principle underlying Article 12, yet some respondents thought that the ability to form an opinion was a higher threshold than an ability to form a view.

The following comments explain this perception:

> What is an opinion? It is not necessarily a 'preference'. It has to do with formal, logical views. Showing by behaviour is not the same as forming an opinion – it's showing a feeling. Opinion is a balanced recognition of all aspects. Views are a bit different; more akin to wishes. Children can form a view quite young; an infant can form a view that it doesn't want any more food. [psychologist]

> In most care and protection instances, children can have a good idea and can offer a view. Whether they can offer an opinion is another question – it depends what it is about. If a child can talk, they can offer some sort of view. [social worker]

> We should distinguish between feelings and a reasoned opinion. We should be trying to seek views. [child welfare organisation]

It is important to note that the official text of Article 12 speaks of views rather than opinions. Given the perception of some that they represent different levels of ability, it is advisable to cultivate the habit of using the correct, official terminology.

5.5.2 *Presumption of Ability at a Specified Age*

Whilst some commented that all children have views and can express them in varying ways, most respondents recognised that there were some issues connected with ascertaining whether a child was capable of forming a view.

Respondents were asked whether it would be helpful to have a benchmark concerning the ability to form a view in the form of a presumption at a particular age. There was an interesting division of opinion between lawyers and non-lawyers. Lawyers tended to favour a benchmark with suggested ages ranging from 8 to 12 years. Non-lawyers tended to argue that there should be no presumption. The view of non-lawyers may be represented by the following quote from an employee of a child welfare organisation:

> There should be no presumption regarding age. Even very young children have views and opinions. [Cf. Murray's and Trevorthaw's research on babies' views of the world.] Their views may not be articulate, but that does not diminish their validity. It is important that we do not confuse validity with accuracy.

The lawyers' view may be represented by a statement by a solicitor to the effect that: 'We need some recognised benchmark, but not at the expense of a flexible approach'.

This division seems less surprising when one considers that lawyers are concerned with the participation of children in formal processes when a positive decision must be made about whether to involve them. Their responses were probably also influenced by the fact that interviews were conducted in a period during which a new statute was passed for Scotland (the Children (Scotland) Act 1995) which states at various points that 'a child 12 years of age or more shall be presumed to be of sufficient age and maturity to form a view'. This is specifically stated to be without prejudice to the rights of younger children. The practical import of this provision is that, if a child of 12 years or more is excluded from participation, the onus will be on the person excluding the child to justify his or her action.

5.5.3   *Disability*

Some respondents referred to complications surrounding the participation of children with special needs. A social worker commented: 'It is more difficult to know with children with disabilities. In care and protection cases, because we need to be as thorough as we can, we use the expertise of psychologists and psychiatrists where there are dilemmas.'

And psychologist commented: 'I would want to think that weight would be given to non-verbally expressed views for disabled and younger children.'

5.5.4   *Who Should Assess Ability to Form a View?*

There was a consensus to the effect that assessment of ability to form a view should not be over-professionalised. Parents and other carers might be appropriate persons in some contexts, although one would have to be alert to situations in which the interests of the child and parent might conflict. In that situation a separate advocate for the child with some training in child development might be needed. This did not necessarily mean a psychologist or psychiatrist. This kind of expertise should be more generalised throughout different professional groups. The following are some of the comments made by respondents from different professional backgrounds:

> A general ability to assess how children speak and draw should be encouraged, with professional expertise in borderline cases. [social worker]

> There is a need for some training for all – but it should be passed on to a professional in some cases. If there is a problem – get psychological advice. [sheriff]

> I wouldn't want to say that all cases needed an expert. People who are themselves healthy, emotionally well balanced and feel affection towards the child should be able to do this. Assessment of ability to form views depends on understanding children and child development without being an expert. A parent who understands child development, is sensitive to the child's needs, affectionate and familiar with the child could perform this task. Some parents are unable to do this and an expert might be required. [psychologist]

It shouldn't be a case of limiting the ability to assess to one class of people, for example solicitors or social workers. There should, within each professional grouping, be some people with a recognised qualification which would equip them for this task. [solicitor]

A warning note was expressed by a sheriff:

A child might say it has an opinion. Whether it has formed an opinion or is expressing one presented to it might be more difficult to ascertain. It might have been heavily influenced by others.

An analysis of the issues was provided by a psychologist along the following lines:

If a statement of preference is regarded as a view (for example 'I want to stay with my dad.'), lots of people could make the assessment. If you say that a view has to be logically related to reasons, you might want someone to spend more time with the child to investigate the reasons and the child's conceptual framework. The third stage would be ascertaining whether they were reasonable reasons. Therefore:

Stage 1. A statement of preference – could be identified by most people.

Stage 2. The reasons behind the statement – the conceptual framework – might require a psychological assessment.

Stage 3. Would be determining whether the child understands the issues and whether the child's conclusions are reasonably related to the framework. Adults might agree that the child has stated a reason, but conclude that it is not a reasonable reason.

5.5.5   Conclusion

The ability to form a view is probably best identified with Stage 1 of the process described above. The general feeling was that this did not need the services of an expert. Some generalised training for all who might work with children was desirable. In cases of doubt, especially where a learning difficulty or disability was involved, the services of an expert would be helpful.

The next question respondents were asked is more relevant to Stages 2 and 3 outlined above.

5.6 How are the Views to be Weighed with Reference to the Child's Maturity?

Respondents to the survey were asked about possible difficulties in assessing the maturity of the child and the weight to be given to the child's views.

Some of the responses echoed those given to the previous question, although it was recognised that this was a more complex task. What factors should one take into account as an indication of maturity? A lawyer commented:

> It's a different task. You need something to measure views by. But what is meant by maturity? Does it mean being sensible and not stamping one's feet? There are some adults I wouldn't consider mature, but I wouldn't dismiss their views.

A social worker asked:

> Do we talk of intellectual and/or emotional, personal maturity. How is this influenced by personality?

Another respondent from a child welfare agency noted that, added to maturity was the question of emotional vulnerability:

> A single parent died leaving two children aged 12 and 5. The younger one had clear views on what arrangements should be made for him. The older one had more difficulty expressing this, so the adults took the responsibility for the decision. He was basically opting out of expressing views.

The maturity of the person making the assessment was also important. A social worker commented:

> You wouldn't need a particular professional background, but you would want people without preconceived notions and very much in touch with themselves. They would need some training.

In some cases, parents or carers might be well placed to make this assessment, although they might need professional advice as a back-up. A social worker from a voluntary organisation suggested that the person making the assessment should be:

> a person skilled in the processes of communication with children and able to win their respect and confidence. I would want to include people 'close'

to the child as being by definition skilled in communicating with that particular child.

However, a voluntary organisation expressed a warning note:

> While the parents/carers may be the best people to judge, they may be 'emotionally unavailable' to their child and therefore unable or unwilling to hear the child's opinion.

It was felt impractical and, by some, unnecessary to suggest a psychological assessment in every case. Was there then a case for identification of skilled persons with more knowledge and objectivity than parents, but less specialist expertise than psychologists, to perform this task?

A psychologist commented:

> Assessing maturity is not difficult for a skilled practitioner, such as a psychologist or psychiatrist. Social workers are not sufficiently instructed in child development, although they may have a great deal of practical experience. You might want to know the child's IQ. The child might look to the bare eye as though functioning as a normal seven-year-old, when he was, in fact, functioning as a five-year-old. It would, however, be unrealistic to expect a psychological assessment in every case. It would be possible to give some guidelines and parameters to others making an assessment, for example the significance of a child's view changing rapidly in half an hour. Training could improve their skills substantially, including helping them to recognise difficulties and get extra help.

Training emerged as an important issue. A worker with a voluntary organisation was concerned that, without adequate training, those responsible for making this assessment might, for example, omit to take account of the child's natural response to stress in matters involving parental separation. This might affect their assessment of the child's maturity. However, several respondents emphasised that training should be diffused amongst professional groups rather than limited to one particular group.

Having made some assessment of the maturity of the child, how does one set about making sure the child's views are given appropriate weight in the decision-making process? Formal processes might in practice, if not in principle, be tokenistic as regards taking the child's views into account in accordance with the assessment of maturity. An experienced children's panel member commented that it was difficult for adults to allow the voice of a child to supersede that of an adult. An example was cited of a case in which a 14-year-old girl was expressing clear views. However:

> The parents were arguing on the basis of 'this is my child'. Adults empathise with adults. There is a temptation to give less weight to the child's views, because most of us who are parents are protective of our children. Panel members recognise that children can be very articulate, but a lot of parents have the view that 'these are our weans and we will tell them what to do' – even if they have no actual control.

A solicitor expressed the view that some Sheriffs might also take a tokenistic approach.

5.6.1 *Conclusion*

Both in relation to assessment of maturity and in ensuring that appropriate weight was given to the child's views, suggestions were made about persons who might perform these tasks. These were variously referred to as safeguarders, guardians and advocates. The consensus was that there was no need to identify any particular professional background as a qualification for this post. However, those charged with assessing the child's maturity and representing the implications of that to the decision-making forum should be mature in themselves and trained in child development and in communication with children and young people, including particular groups, such as adolescents or those with special needs, who present difficulties for some adults.

5.7 Can Welfare ever Override Participation?

Respondents to the survey were asked whether there were any situations in which even inviting or facilitating participation by a child might be harmful to the child's welfare. Were there situations in which concern for the child's welfare might justify completely excluding a child from participation?

Some respondents replied that they could think of no circumstance in which a child should be completely excluded from participation in order to protect their interests. There was a perception that, if we really tried, we could find appropriate mechanisms. There was a suggestion that if we allowed a loophole, it would be misused. A sheriff suggested that it might be very easy to 'talk yourself into' not allowing a child to participate if that facility was available. On the other hand, whilst he himself could not envisage circumstances in which a child should be completely cut out from a decision, he commented: 'But there will be some. Don't tie us down too much'.

A psychologist referred to a case in which a 13-year-old girl had a degenerative illness. She was blind, used a wheelchair and was showing signs of dementia. She did not understand what was happening to her, and her parents refused to allow the medical staff to tell her. The psychologist felt that the information could have been fed to the girl gradually in a supportive way. She would have welcomed the existence of a clear and absolute right of the child to know which could have been put before the parents. Having said this, the psychologist also called for a degree of flexibility.

There was also a perception that, as we were in practice far from an ideal situation in terms of facilitating participation in an appropriate, unharmful way, we might have to acknowledge that inviting participation might in fact be harmful, even though it should not be. This ambivalence was expressed by a respondent from a voluntary organisation who, whilst acknowledging that: 'If decisions are being made about children, particularly in separation and divorce, it is crucial that children don't feel that decisions are being made over them'. nevertheless expressed some misgivings about putting that ideal into practice:

> I would want to say that there should not ever be a situation in which children are completely excluded, but I could see there would be cases in which actually implementing that could cause difficulties, particularly because parents are still trying to catch up on thinking about children's rights. This can apply also to medical issues. Children's and parents' interests are so intermeshed that, even if the motivation of the parent is protection of the parent, that has an impact on the child's interests.

One situation was referred to in which a social work respondent felt that children should not be involved. This was where authorities considered that action must be taken to protect a child from possible significant harm if allowed to remain at home along with a suspected abuser. The Children (Scotland) Act 1995 introduced a new exclusion order that would allow local authorities to apply to the court for authority to exclude an alleged abuser from the home instead of removing the child. The social worker commented:

> We need to be careful about exclusion orders. Involvement could add to the child's guilt about 'blowing the gaff', because the child might now feel responsible for the adult having to leave the house. The child needs to be involved in the decision about the exclusion and why it is happening, but should not be party to that decision. You could give the child the opportunity to say something if they wanted, but not press them.

This comment distinguishes between 'involvement' and participation, with the implication that the child might be allowed to express a view, without being expected to do so.

A psychologist took the matter a little further:

> It might be justifiable to exclude a child if the child is going to feel distraught and responsible by having directly made some statement of preference. Whilst no decision should be made without full account being taken of the child's position and feelings, it is always possible to get the information another way. Children mustn't be made to feel responsible and therefore shouldn't be asked directly. Even if they are told that it is not their decision, they might still feel responsible.

The implication of this is that in situations involving emotional conflict, the child might be asked about their feelings in general, rather than engaged on the subject actually under debate by adults. Our assurances that they are not responsible for the decision might hold little weight if a child has complied with a request to state a preference on a matter on which adults are in conflict.

5.7.1 Conclusion

The request for an element of flexibility mentioned by some respondents sits uneasily with the insistence on participation as a right. Indeed this tension between a rights-based approach and a discretionary one was evident in the responses of some of the individuals interviewed. In view of the benefits to be gained through the practical impact of a positive right to be involved, and the dangers of misuse of any built-in exceptions, the conclusion might be that there should be some exceptional provisions derogating from the general principle, which it should not be made easy to access.

5.8   Forced Participation

Respondents were asked about participation issues arising in their own fields of interest or employment which required to be addressed or considered. Whilst responses to these are mostly more appropriately considered under other headings, one which does perhaps require separate treatment is the question of 'forced participation'. A social worker commented: 'Some young people don't want to hear at all – they don't want to come'. This view was also expressed by a psychologist who said: 'Sometimes children don't want to be at meetings but feel 'egged on' because it is expected of them'.

When the young people were asked whether they should be forced to attend meetings, they felt strongly that this should not happen. One young person described how she was physically restrained by care staff and forced to attend a care review, where she was held down on the seat to stop her leaving. Indications of forced attendance also surfaced in interviews with social workers, where some dubiety about the practice was expressed.

5.8.1   Conclusion

Article 12 of the UN Convention is about rights and opportunities rather than obligations of children. In Scotland, the Children (Scotland) Act 1995 is generally at pains to qualify references to the child's views by adding 'if he wishes to express them'. On the other hand, there is a possibility of children being forced to attend children's hearings. This may be a relic of the juvenile justice origins of the hearing system, and a philosophy of being held to account for your actions. Within that context, it might be acceptable. It sits less easily with a philosophy of care and protection.

5.9 Suggested Changes to Law, Policy and Practice

Respondents were invited to make suggestions for changes to law, policy and practice which would facilitate appropriate participation by children in matters affecting them. The following is a distillation of suggestions made.

5.9.1 Principle

There should be an operational presumption that children be invited to express their views in matters affecting them. Where meetings are to be held, there should be a presumption that children may attend, although they should not necessarily be forced to attend. This means that any exclusion of children and young people against their wishes, or without their knowledge, needs to be positively justified.

5.9.2 Education

There should be more public education on children's rights, so that a climate is created in which it is taken for granted that children participate and are given as much information as possible. Adults may have to be taught how to listen to children and how to seek their opinion without loading all the responsibility on to them. This applies both to parents and professionals. Professionals may also require training in the skill of communicating with children.

Training should include awareness of underlying pressures at a meeting. For example, it was suggested that the fact that a child is present at a meeting increases the pressure on adults to come to a decision. They might fear that the child will feel let down if, after all the preparation, no decision is reached.

Adults should also be encouraged to be wary of mechanisms that might appear to produce easy answers to the participation of children.

Whilst the new Scottish ability to exclude a parent from a meeting in order to allow the child to speak in private has generally been welcomed, adults need to know that this is not a 'soft option', but one that could lead to tensions and difficulties.

5.9.3   Culture

Managers of social work forums, such as reviews, and care planning and child protection meetings, should ensure that the environment established through good practice encourages the involvement of children.

A psychologist made the point that children are not equal partners and never will be. If they are attending with teachers, and so on, it might be impossible for them to overcome their feelings about that relationship.

A worker from a voluntary organisation recommended that we should move away from the 'hostile' atmosphere of adversarial justice, which is not child-centred and which creates an atmosphere which makes it difficult for a child to express views with confidence.

5.9.4   System

A sheriff expressed the opinion that the majority of divorces don't need court interference. Unless there is evidence to the contrary, they should proceed on the basis that parents have fulfilled their responsibility to involve their children. He indicated that where he had raised the question of getting the views of the child, the application for custody or access had simply been dropped. He did not know what was happening there. It seemed to him that, when pushed, parents realised that they didn't need a court order.

He suggested that, in any divorce situation, whether or not an order regarding the child was being sought, an appropriate notice should be served on the child, with a slip which gave the child the opportunity to return something to the court expressing a view, even if it was to the effect that he or she did not want to say anything.

There were a few weighty opinions in favour of 'root and branch surgery' to allow the legal system to accommodate the participation of children. A solicitor suggested that what was required was a new 'custom built process'. It would be important in this new system to avoid exposing children to inappropriate knowledge of adult problems. A psychologist commented that if the system resulted in children receiving inappropriate information, then that would be a denial of the right of a child to be a child.

Some flexibility would be required within the system to ensure that the needs of individual children could be met.

5.9.5   *Procedural Empowerment*

There were a number of comments on the need to empower children and young people to understand what is going on and to express their views. There are various possibilities built into this area:

- initial advice;
- a person to help them speak but not speak for them;
- a person to help them to write their own reports;
- a person to safeguard their interests;
- a person to advocate their views;
- wider advocacy role, not restricted to proceedings;
- preparation for meetings; and
- monitoring the efficacy of procedures.

5.9.6   *Initial Advice*

A child might be aware that decisions were being made and might wish to discuss his or her own position regarding them. A child might even have received formal notice about proceedings affecting him or her. Where should the child go for initial advice?

The availability of initial advice can be crucial in the realisation of children's rights. A children's panel member referred to the procedure by which children appearing before children's hearings receive a piece of paper informing them of their right to bring a representative, and asked 'What does that mean to a seven-year-old'?

Whilst some might use existing facilities such as law centres or advice agencies, it was suggested that the word 'law' was intimidating. There might be a need for a more accessible and generalised source of help and support.

A sheriff suggested that there might be designated a duty teacher in every school to deal with these issues, similar to those currently designated to deal with child protection issues. A children's panel member suggested the establishment of a Child Welfare Commission encompassing this remit.

5.9.7 *Person to Help them to Speak but not Speak for them*

A social worker also acting as a safeguarder set out the case for the appointment of Child Participation Facilitators, rather than advocates, for those young people who were well able to speak for themselves, but might need some help in ensuring that the correct space was made for them to do this. She acknowledged that others would prefer someone to speak for them. What was required was a flexible, but informed approach.

5.9.8 *Person to Help them Write their own Reports*

Two respondents working within the children's hearing system referred to the benefits to be gained from children writing their own reports for a children's hearing. The practice already existed and was increasing. It was noted that children who produce their own reports feel good about it. It was particularly helpful for those children who were reluctant to say much at hearings or for those who had something to say which, because of fear, they did not want the carer or parent to know. It was important that any changes to laws regarding access to reports preserved the current ability to withhold that information.[3]

A sheriff referred to a case concerning a child in which he had asked the child to send him a letter stating her views. In that case it had been a successful tactic.

Children might need some help from an independent person in writing their reports. Again, it was suggested that a teacher might be appropriate, in some, but not all, cases. A Child Welfare Commission might also fulfil this role.

5.9.9   A Person to Safeguard their Interests

A more traditional method of ensuring that the interests of children are represented in formal proceedings is by the appointment of an independent person to undertake that role. In Scotland, a court might appoint a safeguarder, curator, reporting officer or matrimonial reporter. The title and role of the person varies according to the legal authority for the appointment. Some of these roles have a clearer remit than others.

Safeguarders were first appointed within the children's hearing system in 1985. Whilst they were initially very little used, there has been an increased interest in them in the past few years. This interest was reflected in the responses to the survey. A solicitor and former safeguarder commented: 'Safeguarders don't really know what they are doing. Responsibility is often unloaded onto them in difficult cases'.

Whilst welcoming a wider use of safeguarders, a children's panel member emphasised that this must be backed up by training and clarification of expectations of them, with regard, for example, to the production of reports and attendance at children's hearings.

A sheriff reported that he would like to see safeguarders 'beefed up'. The role should not be limited to one professional group, such as social workers or solicitors.

An employee of a child welfare organisation said there should be: 'safeguarders in more proceedings to facilitate children's participation. If the child disagrees with the safeguarder, there should be an additional person appointed to put the child's views forward'.

5.9.10   Person to Advocate their Views

This might be a solicitor. A solicitor with experience of working with child clients pointed out some of the personal and practical considerations in taking on this kind of work: 'Am I qualified to deal with this issue? How will the child get to the office? Should I ask the parents to bring him? Should I be directly in contact with the parent? How do you take instructions from children?'

5.9.11   Wider Advocacy Role, not Restricted to Proceedings

Persons currently appointed to safeguard the interests of children have a narrow remit connected with the proceedings. A social worker suggested that there was a case to be made for a wider advocacy role; this could involve checking on the accuracy of information kept about a child. Files, he said, were often wrong and full of contradictions. They needed to be constantly revised.

5.9.12   Preparation

A psychologist emphasised that children needed to be prepared for meetings. Information should be screened and one should not assume that, because a child was there, he or she was party to the information. Before a meeting, at least one responsible adult should get a good feel of what is going to be discussed and decide whether the child should be present. Where the child is not going to be present, the meeting needs to discuss who is going to tell the child and how the decision will be imparted to him or her. The child needs to know that information too.

5.9.13   Monitoring

A voluntary organisation working with children asked: 'How do we ensure that adults <u>do</u> listen to children and take account of their opinions?'

An employee of another voluntary organisation said there was: 'an urgent need for a commission or ombudsman for children'.

Notes

1. In Scotland, decisions about compulsory measures of care for children are made by a lay tribunal of three, known as a 'children's hearing', and drawn from a local 'children's panel' of specially trained members of the public. Children may

be referred on a number of grounds. These include offending behaviour towards a child and offending behaviour by a child.

2. The reporter is the official responsible for receiving and investigating concerns about a child and placing the case before a children's hearing.

3. Since the survey was conducted, a new provision has been enacted which obliges the reporter to pass on to parents any report which he gives to members of the children's hearing. This provision, which is now found in the Children's Hearings (Scotland) Rules 1996, came into force on 1 October 1996. It was considered necessary to achieve compliance with a decision of the European Court of Human Rights in the case of *McMichael* v *UK Government*. It means that children's reports will not remain private.

Chapter 6

◆

A Framework for a Child-Centred System

6.1   Recap

Chapter 2 of this book explored the text of the UN Convention on the Rights of the Child and the thinking of the drafters. It concluded that, whereas ascertaining a child's views was an essential part of determining where the child's interests lay, the child's right to participate was not qualified by protective considerations. The drafters drew back from any attempt to make the rights set out in the Convention subject to a welfare test. They recognised that this would open the door to a creeping abrogation of the rights of children.

(This approach was supported by the comments of some respondents to the survey quoted in Chapter 5, who acknowledged that adults might misuse an interests-based qualification if it was available to them, partly through concern, and partly because it would make life easier for them.)

The approach of the drafters of the Convention has been carried through into the work of the Committee on the Rights of the Child, which was set up to monitor implementation of the Convention. They emphasise that the rights of children are true rights inhering in them as individuals, and not to be conceded at the discretion of parents or the state.

They consistently decry attempts to avoid or dilute the full implications of the child's right to participate. Poland's protective approach to participation of children in proceedings was criticised as opening the door to subjective interpretations which gave little weight to the actual wishes and feelings of the child. On the other hand, the Committee is not in favour of indiscriminate approaches which appeared to grant virtual autonomy at an early age without investigation of the character of the issue involved and the maturity of the child. They sounded a cautionary note about the freedom of Swedish children to seek legal and medical advice from about the age of seven without parental consent.

The conclusions must be that the interests of children are not to be regarded as an excuse for denying them participation; nor can a simplistic approach to the rights of children justify avoiding the task of investigating the mode of participation and extent of control which is appropriate for an individual child.

The conclusion from Chapter 2 was that children who are capable of forming views have a right to participate in decisions regarding all matters affecting them. That right is an absolute one, although the interests of children are relevant in determining the mode in which it is to be exercised.

Chapter 3 demonstrated the current lack of principle and consistency in the approach of states party to facilitating participation of children in terms of the UN Convention. This demonstrated a need for further guidance on the matter.

Chapter 4 considered the provisions of the 1995 European Convention on the Exercise of Children's Rights, which aims to help members of the Council of Europe fulfil their obligations under the UN Convention, and to achieve a measure of consistency amongst its members. It concluded that the European Convention was of limited use and that adherence to it might lead to the UN Convention being undermined.

Whilst some guidance would be helpful, one must question the practicality of the Council of Europe's aim of achieving consistency amongst its members, given the current variety of philosophy and basic framework throughout Europe. An inquisitorial system pursuing the best interests of the child as its primary objective will require different procedural mechanisms than an adversarial process between adults where issues about the child are not the sole subject of the proceedings. It is of interest that many respondents to the survey reported in Chapter 6 were of the opinion that the interests of the child could not be served in the latter context. Where that situation existed, there would be merit in seeking to change the model altogether.

The rest of this chapter aims to set out a framework for participation of children, incorporating the principles of the UN Convention, noting and at times transcending the provisions of the European Convention, and taking into account the concerns of young people and professionals, which were expressed in the course of the survey. Whilst decision-making processes are generally referred to as 'meetings', this should be understood as applying also to judicial processes unless the contrary is indicated.

Parts of this framework replicate the conclusions of earlier sections of this book. In this chapter, they are placed within a wider context and represented as the author's own conclusions.

6.2 A Framework for Participation

6.2.1 The Right to Participate

The child's right to participate should not be qualified by considerations of the child's interests. Adults cannot deny children the possibility of participation on the ground that involvement in existing decision-making processes would be damaging to a child. It is the task of adults to devise a system which facilitates appropriate participation of children.

Commitment to the Convention requires states to set about this task as a matter of urgency. Given that most will be starting with systems that are not child-friendly, the following question must arise: what should states do in the period between ratification of the Convention and establishment of a new system that conforms with it? Should they extend to children the right to participate in current processes, even if it is felt this might be unhelpful or even damaging to the child?

It is submitted that this simplistic approach would not be helpful to children and should not be regarded as an essential implication of ratification of the Convention. Rather, states should audit existing processes and determine whether and how existing processes could be modified or replaced to accommodate the participation of children, as a step towards full compliance with the Convention's provisions. This might, in the short term, involve the provision of age-appropriate information and personal supports to the child, as well as a sifting process to ensure that no individual child will be damaged by involvement in any particular process.

This means there would be a two-stage approach to implementation, with selective interim measures operating during the period when a comprehensive approach was being considered and established.

6.2.2 The Threshold Condition and the Weighing Process

Article 12.1 of the UN Convention states that a child shall be entitled to participate once he or she is 'capable of forming his or her own views'. The views of the child should then be taken into account and given due weight 'in accordance with the age and maturity of the child'.

There are two tasks involved in compliance with this Article. Someone must ascertain whether the child is capable of forming views, and someone must assess the maturity of the child and the weight to be given to the views expressed.

Whilst it is recognised that the second task is more complex than the first, it would be excessive to demand a psychological or psychiatric test of all children involved in making decisions. It would be preferable if knowledge about child development and the skill of communicating with children were more diffused throughout the population. Not only would this help parents in their general parenting role, but it would equip them to perform this task as part of their parental responsibility.

There should be specific training in these matters for all adults working with children. This includes, not only teachers and others traditionally associated with children, but others such as lawyers, judges, doctors and advice workers.

This approach would mean that there would be many options for assessing these matters, which could be chosen according to the requirements of the situation. Training ought also to include an awareness of indicators that the matter required a more complex assessment, in which case, a psychologist could be called upon to perform it.

Within legal processes, those called upon to represent the interests of the child might be allocated this task. This would free those representing the child's views to concentrate on that perspective. Those charged with assessing the child's maturity and representing the implications of that to a formal decision-making forum should be mature in themselves and trained in child development and in communication with children and young people, including particular groups, such as adolescents or those with special needs, who present difficulties for some adults.

6.2.3   The Presence of the Child at the Decision-making Process

In principle, the presence of the child is neither a necessary nor a sufficient condition of participation.

This means that ratification of the Convention does not oblige states to permit the presence of the child. However, the significance of actual presence varies from forum to forum and different approaches to the issue are advisable.

The presence of the child will be more significant as an aspect of participation when the forum is one open to dialogue, with the expectation that this will affect the outcome. It may be less significant in formal legal processes. It may also be less appropriate when the discussion is a preparatory one at an early stage of exploring options. This would apply for example to early meetings of parents in the process of family mediation. There was a strong plea from respondents to the survey for parents to be given some space to speak together without the child being present.

Where children are not given a right to be present, the system must allow them the opportunity to have their views heard through a report or a representative, and to challenge any decision based upon information to which they were not party, and which might, for example, have emerged at the meeting.

In many instances, it will be more satisfactory to devise the system on the expectation that the child will be present. This would also be more acceptable to young people who resent being excluded from meetings called to decide upon their future.

Where children are expected to attend meetings it is essential that:

- They are prepared for the meeting and given access to appropriate information.
- They are helped to consider beforehand how they might best express their views. Some young people might welcome the accompaniment of a trusted person; others might be helped to write their own reports.
- They are told in advance who else is likely to be at the meeting, so that inhibiting factors can be identified and addressed. There should be a possibility of excluding other persons whose presence might inhibit the child in order to allow the child to speak freely.
- Before the meeting, a responsible person should consider the information which will be available and the matters which might emerge at the meeting and take steps to ensure as far as possible that the meeting will proceed in a way that meets the needs of the child.
- Adults who attend the meetings should be trained to avoid jargon and be aware of the impact on the child of what they say.
- At the meeting a responsible person should be charged with monitoring its progress with regard to the effect on the child, and taking any steps necessary to serve the interests of the child.
- At the conclusion of the meeting, the proposed decision must be discussed with the child to ensure that he or she fully understands it and, if the child wishes, makes their agreement or disagreement clear.
- After the meeting, a responsible person is charged with de-briefing the child. This may be done at the end of the meeting, but in some cases, it may be more appropriate to follow it up with the child later once the emotional impact of the meeting has subsided.

Children should not normally be forced to attend meetings. Article 12 of the UN Convention is about rights and opportunities rather than obligations of children. Forced attendance may be appropriate in a juvenile justice system, on the basis that children, like others, should be held to account for their actions. It sits less easily with a philosophy of care and protection and with normal civil processes to which they are not party.

6.2.4 Access to Information

True participation involves access to the information on which the decision will be based. This does not mean that all the information in a process should be given to a child. Some of it will not be relevant to the child's contribution. Knowledge of some of it might be harmful to the child if not given at an appropriate time and place, and if the child has not been prepared to receive it.

The following principles aim to assist in facilitating access to appropriate information:

- The presumption should be in favour of passing on all relevant information to a child participating in a decision.
- There should be a possibility of withholding information – temporarily at least – in the interests of the child.
- Information should be sifted by a responsible person to determine what it is relevant for a child to know and whether knowledge of it might be damaging to a child.
- A responsible person should ascertain what a child already knows about the situation.
- In some situations, the 'responsible person' will be the child's parent or carer. There must be a method of challenging the parent's decision to withhold information if others feel that the child should have it. In formal situations, or where there is a conflict of interest, the deciding body or an independent person should be allocated this task.
- If it is felt some information might be damaging to a child, consideration should be given as to how it could be presented in a way that would make it easier for the child to accept without damage.
- Before a meeting which a child will attend, a responsible person should scan available information, consider what a child already knows, identify any points of difficulty and recommend arrangements to address them.
- Wherever possible, meetings should be arranged within a timescale that allows the proceedings to be continued to allow a child to be informed and counselled on relevant information that might come to light during it. Difficulties could be encountered if an order is required to be made or renewed within a tight timescale.
- If information is withheld from a child in the course of judicial or administrative proceedings, an independent person should be appointed to represent the interests of the child in those proceedings, with access to the information denied to the child.
- Information should be presented to children in a way that is meaningful to them.

6.2.5   *The Representation of Children*

As was mentioned earlier in this book, a child-centred decision-making system might include some of the following elements:

- accessible and comprehensible initial advice for children;
- a person to help them to speak, but not speak for them;
- a person to help them to write their own reports;
- a person to safeguard their interests;
- a person to advocate their views; and
- provision of advocacy in a broader sense, not restricted to proceedings.

The issue of representation is crucial. The UN Convention sets out principles about participation; it does not give much guidance on how they should be put into practice. The provision of a 'representative' is one of a number of options referred to in Article 12.2 as a means of respecting the right to be heard. There is no reference to a person who might represent the interests of the child. This responsibility rests with the decision-making forum as a whole.

Nevertheless, in adversarial systems at least, the decision will be made by that forum on the basis of information presented to it. It is essential that an independent person is charged with investigating and presenting information aimed at securing the child's best interests. It is desirable that that person, in an adversarial system, be given the opportunity to cross-examine parties to the proceedings.

As has been noted, many systems conjoin the role of representative of the child's interests and views. It is expected that a person with a remit to represent the interests of the child will pay heed to the child's views. This may seem to be in conformity with the thinking of the drafters of the Convention, who regarded ascertainment of views as an essential part of determining interests. However, this removes a lot of influence from the court on to the representative. It is submitted that it is quite a different thing to represent the child's views and to present them in the context of a report that is recommending something else. At the very least, a child who disagrees with the conclusion of his or her representative should have the possibility of instructing someone else to advocate his or her views and nothing else.

Against this it is argued that, not only does such double representation involve extra expense, it is also liable to confuse the child and overload him or her with people wishing to discuss matters and ask questions.

A compromise position might be achieved whereby a representative is appointed to represent the child's interests, while taking account of his or her views. But, in this case, a child who disagreed with this person should be able to instruct a separate representative to advocate his or her views.

One of the justifications for making representation of interests the basic building block is that some children will not want to take responsibility for influencing the decision in matters where they may have torn loyalties. The representative of interests can act as a buffer in this respect. The child then has the option of having an advocate of his or her views.

Whilst this system of representation is a more extensive commitment than that required by the European Convention, it is consistent with it and arguably represents a higher standard.

6.2.6 Monitoring

The UN Committee on the Rights of the Child has consistently called upon states to set up monitoring mechanisms, and criticised those who have not.

Given the concerns expressed about the participation of children, and the likelihood that most states will have to proceed initially on the basis of interim measures, it is crucial that a monitoring system is established. This should relate to both formal and informal processes. Informal processes may require particular attention as they are subject to less scrutiny. Some respondents to the survey suggested that a Child Welfare Commission or Children's Rights Commissioner might be appointed to undertake this task.

It would also be valuable for states to have an international mechanism for comparing the measures adopted to implement Article 12. The right to participate is acknowledged as the most novel and radical contribution of the UN Convention on the Rights of the Child. There is an understandable fear about entering new waters and exposing children to untried processes. We dislike the idea of experimenting on our children. It would be more practical and ethical to exchange information about ideas already tried.

6.3   Conclusion

A serious commitment to the principle of children's participation needs to be backed up by a public education programme. A truly serious commitment would involve a radical rethink of the decision-making systems in relation to children: of culture, expectations and procedures. The timescale of proceedings, the availability and form of information and the organisation of any event should all be arranged in the light of the needs of the child and the reality of participation by children.

If children are truly to be regarded as human beings and citizens in their own right, the professionals who provide the framework within which that system operates must become accustomed to considering children of all ages as consumers and clients. Children should not be seen as deviations from the adult norm, who can be accommodated only at some inconvenience to adult-centred processes. Their needs and rights must be integrated into the system as a whole.

APPENDIX

Act of Sederunt (Sheriff Court Ordinary Cause Rules) 1993 – Version 1 – Introduced by the 1993 rules.

FORM F9

Form of intimation in an action which affects a child

Court ref. no.

To (*insert name and address as in warrant*)

You are given NOTICE that in this action, the pursuer craves the court to (*insert details of the crave(s) that affect the child*) which affect you. A copy of the initial writ is attached. If you wish to apply to appear as a party, you must lodge a minute with the sheriff clerk (*insert address of sheriff clerk*) for leave to do so. Your minute must be lodged within 21 days of (*insert date on which intimation was given. N.B. Rule 5.3(2) relating to postal service or intimation*).

Date (*insert date*)

Signed ....

Solicitor for the pursuer ....

NOTE

If you decide to lodge a minute it may be in your best interest to consult a solicitor. The minute should be lodged with the sheriff clerk with the appropriate fee (insert amount) and a copy of this intimation.

IF YOU ARE UNCERTAIN WHAT ACTION TO TAKE you should consult a solicitor. You may be entitled to legal aid depending on your financial circumstances, and you can get information about legal aid from a solicitor. You may also obtain advice from any Citizens' Advice Bureau or other advice agency.

Act of Sederunt (Sheriff Court Ordinary Cause Rules) 1993 – Version 2 – Introduced by an amendment to the 1993 rules effected by the Act of Sederunt (Family Proceedinmgs in the Sheriff Court) 1996.

FORM F9   Rules 33.7(1)(h)

Form of intimation in an action which includes a crave for a section 11 order

PART A   Court Ref. No.

> **This part must be completed by the Pursuer's solicitor in language a child is capable of understanding.**

To   **(1)**

The Sheriff (the person who has to decide about your future) has been asked by **(2)**   to decide:-

   (a) **(3)** and **(4)**

   (b) **(5)**

   (c) **(6)**

If you want to tell the Sheriff what you think about the things your **(2)**   has asked the Sheriff to decide about your future you should complete Part B of this form and send it to the Sheriff Clerk at **(7)** by **(8)**   . An envelope which does not need a postage stamp is enclosed for you to use to return the form.

> **IF YOU DO NOT UNDERSTAND THIS FORM OR IF YOU WANT HELP TO COMPLETE IT you may get help from a SOLICITOR or contact the SCOTTISH CHILD LAW CENTRE ON the FREE ADVICE TELEPHONE LINE ON 0800 317 500.**

If you return the form it will be given to the Sheriff. The Sheriff may wish to speak with you and may ask you to come and see him or her.

NOTES FOR COMPLETION

(1) Insert name and address of child.	(2) Insert relationship to the child of party making the application to court.
(3) Insert appropriate wording for residence order sought.	(4) Insert address.
(5) Insert appropriate wording for contact order sought.	(6) Insert appropriate wording for any other order sought.
(7) Insert address of sheriff clerk.	(8) Insert the date occurring 21 days after the date on which intimation is given. N.B. Rule 5.3(2) relating to intimation and service.
(9) Insert court reference number.	(10) Insert name and address of parties to the action.

PART B

IF YOU WISH THE SHERIFF TO KNOW YOUR VIEWS ABOUT YOUR FUTURE YOU SHOULD COMPLETE THIS PART OF THE FORM

To the Sheriff Clerk, (7)

Court Ref. No. (9)

(10) . . . .

QUESTION (1): DO YOU WISH THE SHERIFF TO KNOW WHAT YOUR VIEWS ARE ABOUT YOUR FUTURE?

(PLEASE TICK BOX)

Yes	
No	

If you have ticked YES please also answer Question (2) *or* (3)

QUESTION (2): WOULD YOU LIKE A FRIEND, RELATIVE OR OTHER PERSON TO TELL THE SHERIFF YOUR VIEWS ABOUT YOUR FUTURE?

(PLEASE TICK BOX)

Yes	
No	

If you have ticked YES please write the name and address of the person you wish to tell the Sheriff your views in Box (A) below. You should also tell that person what your views are about your future.

BOX A: (NAME) . . . .

             (ADDRESS) . . . .

             . . . .

             Is this person:-   A friend? ☐   A relative? ☐

                                A teacher? ☐   Other? ☐

OR

QUESTION (3): WOULD YOU LIKE TO WRITE TO THE SHERIFF AND TELL HIM WHAT YOUR VIEWS ARE ABOUT YOUR FUTURE?

(PLEASE TICK BOX)

Yes	
No	

If you decide that you wish to write to the Sheriff you can write what your views are about your future in Box (B) below or on a separate piece of paper. If you decide to write your views on a separate piece of paper you should send it along with this form to the Sheriff Clerk in the envelope provided.

BOX B: **WHAT I HAVE TO SAY ABOUT MY FUTURE:-**

NAME: . . . .

ADDRESS: . . . .

DATE: . . . .

Survey Questionnaire Form

Glasgow University, Centre for the Study of the Child and Society

Participation by Children in Decision-making

Survey conducted by Kathleen Marshall, Gulbenkian Fellow in Children's Rights

1(a) Do you basically agree with the participation principle set out in Article 12 of the UN Convention on the Rights of the Child?

❑ Yes   ❑ No

1(b) Please give reasons for your answer.

....

....

2(a) Are there circumstances in which adults need to be able to discuss issues relating to the child without the child being present?

❑ Yes   ❑ No

2(b) If yes, please give examples

....

....

2(c) If yes, please explain what you think will happen if this need is not recognised.

....

....

2d Please insert any other comments

....

....

3(a) Is it ever legitimate to withhold relevant information from a child in order to protect the child's interests?

❑ Yes   ❑ No

....

....

3(b) If yes, please give examples.

....

....

3(c)   Who should decide what and when to withhold?

....

....

3(d)   Please insert any comments.

....

....

4(a)   Can you envisage any difficulties in ascertaining whether a child is capable of forming an opinion?

❑   Yes   ❑   No

....

....

4(b)   Who is best qualified to decide?

....

....

4(c)   Should there be a presumption about the age at which a child is regarded as mature enough to form an opinion?

❑   Yes   ❑   No

....

....

4(d)   If yes, what age should it be?

....

4(e)   Please insert any comments

....

....

5(a)   Can you envisage any difficulties in assessing the maturity of the child and the weight to be given to the child's opinion?

❑   Yes   ❑   No

....

....

5(b)   Who is best qualified to make the assessment?

....

....

5(c)   Please insert any comments.

....

....

6(a) Can you envisage situations in which even inviting or facilitating participation by a child might be harmful to the child's welfare?

❑ Yes   ❑ No

....
....

6(b) If yes, please list and justify.

....
....

6(c) Please insert any comments.

....
....

7. Please set out any issues about participation arising in your own field of interest or employment which require to be addressed or considered.

❑ Yes   ❑ No

....
....

8. General Comments/Overflow from previous pages.

....
....

9. Do you wish your comments to remain anonymous?

❑ Yes   ❑ No

Name ....

Designation ....

PLEASE FEEL FREE TO CONTINUE ON A SEPARATE SHEET.

INDEX

118

Published by The Stationery Office and available from:

The Stationery Office Bookshops
71 Lothian Road, Edinburgh EH3 9AZ
(counter service only)
9-10 High Holborn, London WC1V 6HB
(Temporary location until mid-1998)
Fax 0171-831 1326
68-69 Bull Street, Birmingham B4 6AD
0121-236 9696 Fax 0121-236 9699
33 Wine Street, Bristol BS1 2BQ
0117-926 4306 Fax 0117-929 4515
9-21 Princess Street, Manchester M60 8AS
0161-834 7201 Fax 0161-833 0634
16 Arthur Street, Belfast BT1 4GD
01232 238451 Fax 01232 235401
The Stationery Office Oriel Bookshop
The Friary, Cardiff CF1 4AA
01222 395548 Fax 01222 384347

The Stationery Office publications are also available from:
The Publications Centre
(mail, telephone and fax orders only)
PO Box 276, London SW8 5DT
General enquiries 0171-873 0011
Telephone orders 0171-873 9090
Fax orders 0171-873 8200

Accredited Agents
(see Yellow Pages)
and through good booksellers

Printed in Scotland for The Stationery Office Limited J22166, C10, CCN 003093, 10/97